Cambridge Elements ≡

Elements in Politics and Society in East Asia
edited by
Erin Aeran Chung
Johns Hopkins University
Mary Alice Haddad
Wesleyan University
Benjamin L. Read
University of California, Santa Cruz

JAPAN'S NEW INDUSTRIAL POLICY

Gregory W. Noble
University of Tokyo

CAMBRIDGE
UNIVERSITY PRESS

Shaftesbury Road, Cambridge CB2 8EA, United Kingdom

One Liberty Plaza, 20th Floor, New York, NY 10006, USA

477 Williamstown Road, Port Melbourne, VIC 3207, Australia

314–321, 3rd Floor, Plot 3, Splendor Forum, Jasola District Centre,
New Delhi – 110025, India

103 Penang Road, #05–06/07, Visioncrest Commercial, Singapore 238467

Cambridge University Press is part of Cambridge University Press & Assessment,
a department of the University of Cambridge.

We share the University's mission to contribute to society through the pursuit of
education, learning and research at the highest international levels of excellence.

www.cambridge.org
Information on this title: www.cambridge.org/9781009578653

DOI: 10.1017/9781009246552

First published 2025

A catalogue record for this publication is available from the British Library

ISBN 978-1-009-57865-3 Hardback
ISBN 978-1-009-24656-9 Paperback
ISSN 2632-7368 (online)
ISSN 2632-735X (print)

Japan's New Industrial Policy

Elements in Politics and Society in East Asia

DOI: 10.1017/9781009246552
First published online: March 2025

Gregory W. Noble
University of Tokyo

Author for correspondence: Gregory W. Noble, gregory.w.noble@gmail.com

Abstract: Once hailed for implementing an industrial policy so effective that it transformed Japan into a model "developmental state," from the 1980s Japan steadily liberalized its economy and Japanese firms increasingly shifted production abroad via outward foreign direct investment. Yet industrial policy did not just fade away. With the emergence of new competitors in South Korea and Taiwan, and especially the rise of China as a security threat, the Japanese government strove to enhance the viability and competitiveness of Japanese firms as a means to strengthen economic security and reduce reliance on imported energy. Using newly compiled data on Japan's policy apparatus, political environment, and policy challenges, this Element examines how Japan, once an exemplar of "catch up" industrialization, has struggled to "keep up" with new challenges to national economic security, and more briefly considers how its policy evolution compares to those of its East Asian neighbors.

Keywords: political science and international relations, economics, business, sociology, Asian studies

ISBNs: 9781009578653 (HB), 9781009246569 (PB), 9781009246552 (OC)
ISSNs: 2632-7368 (online), 2632-735X (print)

Contents

Preface

Recent years have witnessed a surprising resurgence of industrial policy, the use of government policy to protect and promote specific domestic industries, particularly those seen as crucial to economic growth and national security. Industrial promotion entails choices about which industries merit promotion and can be contrasted to "horizontal" policies such as deregulation or investment tax credits intended to promote growth and productivity across all sectors of the economy. Industrial policy also shapes industry structure, particularly the balance of large, small, and start-up firms. Industrial policy often includes promotion of upstream suppliers, such as providers of steel, glass, and rubber to automobile assemblers, or producers of semiconductors for use in electronic equipment.

Much of the interest in industrial policy has been stimulated by the extraordinary economic transformation of East Asia. A number of scholars and practitioners suggested that Japan's remarkably rapid economic growth after World War II and the rise to global prominence of Japanese companies in such advanced industries as steel, automobiles, and electronics could be attributed in part to industrial policy based on close cooperation between government and business (Kaplan 1972: 113, Johnson 1982). Similar conclusions soon emerged regarding Japan's former colonies South Korea and Taiwan (Amsden 1989, Wade 1990).

Not surprisingly, such contentions aroused fierce opposition from neoclassical economists, who counseled abstention or at most horizontal policies (Beason and Weinstein 1996). By the early 1990s, the bursting of the Japanese financial bubble and the slowdown in growth in South Korea and Taiwan reduced interest in the experience of East Asia, and discussion of industrial policy in the west largely disappeared.

The global financial crisis of 2007–09, however, shook confidence in the Anglo-American model of unrestrained markets, not least because it broke out just as China neared the peak of a run of economic growth even more rapid and sustained than those of its capitalist neighbors, leading to surging exports, a jarring impact on manufacturing employment in advanced countries, and the rise of a much more capable and aggressive Chinese military. Even as ominous cracks emerged over the succeeding decade in the overall pattern of Chinese development, it became clear that industrial policy had contributed to the rise of many strategically significant industries, such as aerospace, solar panels, advanced batteries, electric vehicles, and even some segments of the semiconductor industry (Naughton 2021, Yang 2023). Scholars explored new theoretical rationales and empirical measures for industrial policy (Juhász et al. 2023), while policymakers in the United States and elsewhere strove to devise programs to match or constrain the Chinese threat: Whether or not industrial policy could accelerate overall economic growth, it had clearly contributed to the development of numerous industries important for national security (The White House 2021). American policymakers also urged Japan and other Asian allies and friends to join in efforts to constrain China's strategic and industrial capacity, reduce reliance on strategic imports from China, and promote domestic output of products with implications for national security.

The result was a fundamental transformation of Japanese industrial policy. After steadily declining in intensity and prominence from the 1980s through the 2010s, industrial policy took on a new importance in 2020. The implications of industrial development for national defense and diplomacy, mostly an indirect and secondary concern during the postwar period, suddenly advanced to center stage. The top leadership of the ruling Liberal Democratic Party (LDP) asserted control over a policy arena previously left mainly to bureaucrats and their backbench and mid-rank political supporters.

This Element will trace the transformation of industrial policy in East Asia, including the crucial energy sector, with particular attention to the partial move away from traditional industrial policy toward horizontal policies aimed at enhancing overall flexibility and innovation, and then the more recent shift in emphasis toward economic security. It will examine the policy machinery and political dynamics behind industrial policy, focusing primarily on Japan, but also including brief comparisons to its close neighbors and economic partners South Korea, Taiwan, and China.

1 Introduction

Industrial policy gained fame for protecting and promoting the Japanese economy through a period of extraordinary expansion from the 1950s through the mid-1970s, when Japan largely completed catching up to Europe and the United States. Protection involved tariffs on imports and restrictions on inflows of foreign investment, while promotion included budgetary subsidies and allocations of preferential credit. Over the next two decades, growth slowed, Japanese firms increasingly replaced exports with outward foreign investment, and industrial policy took on a more modest role. From the mid-1990s, two new and potentially contradictory impulses have emerged. First, Japanese policymakers sought to enhance economic flexibility and efficiency by reducing targeting of particular industries in favor of cutting regulation and fostering the growth of new markets for technology and finance. Second, while policymakers have always viewed industrial capabilities as a crucial component of national power, since the

2010s they have reacted to the rise of China and the heightening of tension between China and the United States over trade and security by embracing a more direct and defensive concept of *economic security* (経済安全保障). As a result, after decades of economic liberalization, political reform, and bureaucratic reorganization, a renewed commitment to protecting and promoting domestic firms to enhance economic security reanimated Japanese industrial policy. Making that policy flexible, efficient, and effective, however, has proved to be exceedingly difficult.

Public–Private Cooperation for Industrial Catchup

Industrial policy is difficult to define and measure rigorously, in part because it responds flexibly to the perceived needs of an ever-changing economy, but at its heart is a concern for strategic significance and not just the maximization of comparative advantage and national wealth emphasized by economists (Krugman 1994). Industrial policy cares more about semiconductor chips than potato chips and – particularly in East Asia – it cares about who makes the semiconductor chips:

> Japanese industrial policy aims to protect and promote the competitiveness of domestic firms engaged in strategic activities. The meaning of "strategic" includes economic considerations such as value added, income elasticity of demand, and research intensity, but also can include diplomatic or military significance, international prestige, and maintenance of employment (particularly the "regular" employment characteristic of prime-age male workers). This concern for the survival and strategic competitiveness of domestic firms overlaps with the promotion of economic development, but on occasion may deviate from it. For example ... improving the efficiency of hair salons through relaxation of health regulations might raise productivity and national income, but would have limited strategic significance. (Noble 2021)

In the first three decades after World War II, elite "pilot agencies" led by the Ministry of Finance (MOF) and the Ministry of International Trade and Industry (MITI) employed plentiful policy tools bequeathed by the military and Occupation regimes to promote "catch-up" industrialization (Johnson 1982, Suehiro 2008). They mobilized and coordinated savings and investments through a highly regulated, bank-centered financial system, and controlled allocation of foreign exchange. In consort with industry associations, peak business federations led by Keidanren, and a wide range of policy advisory committees (generically known as *shingikai*), they collected and diffused information, promoted and protected specific industries and products, organized research and development consortia, and assisted firms with industry standards, testing, and verification.

These patterns of public–private cooperation enjoyed strong political support from the long-ruling LDP and a broad (though not unchallenged) social consensus on the priority of economic growth and social stability. Several potentially conflicting motivations guided elite bureaucrats in the economic ministries. First, of course, was the national interest in advancing economic efficiency and technological proficiency. Second was the electoral interests of the LDP, including providing particularistic goodies for localities, declining regions and industries, and small- and medium-sized firms, as well as protection and support for the politically vital agricultural sector. Many of these politically motivated policies were far from economically optimal, but free-market purism was not a politically viable alternative, and evidence suggests that industrial policy mostly managed to avoid providing munificent and open-ended support (Pekkanen 2003).

In addition to pursuing national economic and political goals, ministries had narrower concerns that propelled but also potentially distorted industrial policy. Elite bureaucrats spent virtually their entire careers in individual ministries and those ministries had a strong interest in enhancing their power and prestige. They competed to promote attractive-sounding projects that could stake a claim on new allocations from the government budget, and they maintained close ties with the firms under their jurisdiction, whose cooperation was vital for ensuring the smooth implementation of policy, and for providing cushy jobs for many of the elite bureaucrats in their post-ministry careers, the so-called *amakudari* or "descent from heaven." Monopolization of personnel matters within each ministry impeded cooperation across agencies, frequently criticized in Japan as "vertical administration" (縦わり行政) or siloism.

Mixed motives also characterized the business community. Constrained by the commitment to long-term employment for core male workers and intent on attaining economies of scale to reduce costs, most major Japanese firms placed greater emphasis on gaining market share and ensuring stability than on maximizing profitability. Even as they invested heavily and jockeyed for market share, firms showed a marked preference for cooperation within business groups, industry associations, and the ubiquitous policy deliberation committees. Firms accepted that MITI enjoyed broad jurisdiction and discretion, but they almost always succeeded in blocking excessive interference: "[W]hile the terms of the government-industry equation are constantly disputed, the equation itself, like industrial policy, is non-contentious. Industry resists 'control' (tosei) but regards regulation (chosei) as indispensable; free-market purism is confined to the academy" (Boyd 1986: 85). New entrants and maverick firms that spurned cooperation and challenged mainstream alliances were not unknown, especially before the mid-1960s, but established companies, backed by MITI, typically dominated the policy environment (Noble 1998).

Overall, industrial policy based on public–private cooperation contributed to, or at least did not prevent, extraordinary growth in investment, output, and exports of manufactured goods. Through the 1970s, comparative advantage based on modest wages and relatively high levels of education powered crucial export industries such as textiles and sundries. In industries such as steel, automobiles, and electronics, protection and promotion clearly contributed to endogenous accumulation of skills and eventual attainment of international competitiveness. In other cases, such as retailing and coal mining, politically inspired protection buttressed social stability at the cost of reduced economic efficiency. Whether as catalyst or inhibitor, industrial policy remained ubiquitous (Noble 2021).

To be sure, Japan experienced steady (or at least punctuated) economic liberalization and political reform even during the era of rapid growth, but at first the pace was slow. Economic liberalization that reduced tools available to industrial policymakers began as early as the early 1960s, as Japan prepared to enter the Organisation for Economic Co-operation and Development (OECD), and continued through the 1980s, largely as a response to pressure from Japan's trading partners.

The Transformation of the Economic Environment

The 1980s through the early 2000s brought a major transformation of the economic environment surrounding Japanese firms. Trade friction with the United States intensified as Japanese firms began exporting more capital- and technology-intensive products such as steel, cars, and semiconductors. The Plaza Accord of 1985 led to the revaluation of the yen and other Northeast Asian currencies, spurring investment by Japanese (and other) firms in labor-intensive industries in Southeast Asia and China and greatly contributing (along with "reform and opening" in China) to the rise of China as the dominant economic force in East Asia. In response to the "big bang" financial reforms in Britain and the dismantling of the Bell telephone system in United States, Japan undertook a major reformation (not just deregulation) of regulatory policy in finance and telecommunications, opening the way to an influx of new products and firms and making it easier for Japanese firms to finance and manage global operations (Vogel 1996). An enormous bubble in Japanese land and stock markets broke at the beginning of the 1990s, though it took nearly a decade for the magnitude of the slowdown in growth to become clear.

Trade friction, currency shifts, economic liberalization, and the relative decline of the value of the Japanese market combined to spark a momentous shift from exports to outward foreign direct investment (FDI), led by Japan's famous automobile and electronics industries. The Japanese government and Japanese firms shifted to a much more aggressive use of global, regional, and bilateral investment and trade agreements (Pekkanen 2005). Even agriculture, long the most politically sensitive sector, was the subject of gradual liberalization (Maclachlan and Shimizu 2021). As overseas investments increasingly replaced exports, Japanese trade surpluses shrank and eventually disappeared. In 2000, Japan ran a modest trade surplus of $69 billion and received a net influx of about the same amount ($71 billion) in primary income, mainly returns on overseas investments. By 2022 the trade surplus had turned into a deficit of $159 billion, while net returns on overseas investments surged to $269 billion (World Bank, World Bank). Once a mercantilist, Japan became a rentier, dependent on the receipts from its overseas investments to pay for imports and keep its current account in the black (Katada 2020).

Domestically, Japanese companies focused less on market share and more on profitability and grew more independent of the government and the Japanese market. As they lost ground to South Korean and Chinese firms at the low end, Japanese companies invested more heavily in research and development, applied for more patents, and sought to differentiate their offerings.

The Transformation of the Policy Environment

The policy system also evolved, as electoral and administrative changes in the 1990s reduced the independence and political influence of ministries (Hoshi and Lipscy 2021). Campaign financing reform and revision of the electoral system of the House of Representatives in 1994 strengthened the hand of the prime minister and LDP party center against factions and unruly backbenchers and policy mavens, who had often served as advocates for various ministries.

A major reorganization of the bureaucracy took effect in 2001, merging some ministries, stripping others of part of their jurisdictions, and installing more politicians at the top of the ministries. A major loser was the MOF, which took blame for the expansion and then bursting of the financial bubble and for several tawdry personnel scandals. The new and independent Financial Services Agency (FSA) included staff transferred from MOF but also a major influx of personnel from the private sector. Several other regulatory agencies independent of the ministries followed, covering such areas as information privacy, consumer affairs, and regulation of nuclear power. The biggest winner of the 2001 reorganization was MITI, which gained new responsibilities for the whole economy, as reflected in its new name, the Ministry of Economy, Trade and Industry (METI) (Elder 2003).

The new METI undertook numerous "horizontal" measures intended to increase the productivity and flexibility of the entire market economy, many of them quite different from the protection and promotion of specific domestic industries characteristic of classic "vertical" industrial policy. The METI officials pushed for reform of the company law and promoted revisions to corporate governance, including pressing companies to include more outside directors on their governing boards. They sought to encourage venture capital, private equity, and inward foreign investment, and to smooth the way for mergers and acquisitions. They also encouraged investment in research and development by tightening intellectual property laws and encouraged university researchers to found new start-ups and increase cooperation with established enterprises. The reforms, however, generally sought to increase options available to incumbent firms rather than subject them to "creative destruction."

The 2001 reforms also strengthened the legal and political position of the prime minister and the cabinet. The new Council on Economic and Fiscal Policy (CEFP), which included not only government leaders but also academic economists and private business executives, played a major role in directing economic policy. Eligibility of Diet members for cabinet positions became less dependent on seniority and factional affiliation and more reliant on policy skills and relationship to the prime minister. After civil service reforms in 2014 under Prime Minister Abe Shinzo, the prime minister and the chief cabinet secretary vetted appointments to the top 600 positions in the bureaucracy, thus increasing the responsiveness of elite bureaucrats to the political leadership. The route to top positions in the ministries increasingly included a stint in the Cabinet Secretariat, which expanded from 822 officials in 2000, just before the reforms, to nearly 3,000 in 2018 under Abe (Takenaka 2021: 56–57).

The Reemergence of Economic Weakness and Vulnerability

It is no exaggeration to say that the Japanese political system experienced a fundamental transformation after 2001, becoming far more centralized, less beholden to narrow interest groups, and more attentive to the median voter (Hoshi and Lipscy 2021). Yet despite these massive changes, important continuities remained, not least in industrial policy. If Japanese firms became more sophisticated and globalized, they were still – and in some ways were even more – vulnerable after the bursting of the economic bubble. The employment system continued to rely heavily on core male workers better equipped with firm-specific on-the-job training than on specialized, portable skills. Employment, in turn, still served as the major form of social welfare (Miura 2012). As a result, most firms remained reluctant to carry out major reorganizations, such as selling noncore divisions or merging with other companies, that might require laying off workers. Japanese firms invested less at home and more overseas, but foreigners rarely reciprocated: Japan's slow growth, aging population, and rigid employment systems discouraged inward FDI, a major source of dynamism in China, South Korea, and most other leading industrial economies (Katz 2022). Heavy reliance on a rigid seniority system manned by generalist workers made it difficult for Japanese companies to specialize, innovate, and carry out strategic transformations sufficient to compete with nimbler rivals in the United States, South Korea, Taiwan, and occasionally even China. Start-up activity increased but remained relatively low. In 2021, Japan boasted just six unicorns – start-up companies with a valuation of $1 billion or more – fewer than half as many as India, Singapore, or South Korea, and less than 5 percent of China's total (*Nikkei Asia* June 21, 2022). According to the leading global survey of entrepreneurship activity, "Japan and Iran are among the lowest scores for knowing an entrepreneur, seeing good opportunities, and thinking it easy to start a business" (Hill et al. 2022: 36).

To be sure, by the early 2020s, signs of change began to appear, in part because of the tight labor market resulting from demographic aging. Mergers and acquisitions became more common. Venture capital, new start-ups, and mid-career hires all increased, albeit from a low level (Katz 2023). Variance across firms in strategy, organization, and performance expanded. Prominent firms such as SONY and Panasonic shifted strategic focus from consumer electronics to industrial applications, and from hardware to software and networks. Schaede (2020) argued that these new trends constituted "the business reinvention of Japan" and rendered industrial policy increasingly irrelevant.

These political and business reforms, however, exerted little discernible impact on overall economic performance. Economic growth remained slow and uncertain. Even a massive buildup of public debt was insufficient to pull Japan out of a twenty-year deflation. As wages stagnated, while taxes and social security contributions increased to cope with demographic aging, household consumption actually contracted slightly (Statistics Bureau of Japan). The inability to overcome deflation, the shock of the global financial crisis of 2007–09, and the steady increase in the proportion of workers in irregular jobs combined to create a sense of increasing inequality and pervasive anxiety: "feelings of vulnerability spread across all social strata indicating a precarisation of Japanese society" (Chiavacci and Hommerich 2017: 16).

The contrast with Japan's neighbors was especially striking. Over the first two decades of the twenty-first century, wages in South Korea increased by about one-third, surpassing those of Japan (OECD). China's gross domestic product (GDP) expanded by a factor of 10, leaving it almost three times as large as Japan's (World Bank). Even more striking was the loss of industrial competitiveness. Once the leaders in semiconductors, robots, solar panels, electric vehicles and batteries, and many other products, Japanese firms found themselves challenged or surpassed by rivals from China, South Korea, and Taiwan. Japan's decline was especially shocking in the semiconductor industry, which provides crucial inputs into many other products and industries: "Japanese firms' global share of the semiconductor industry stood at 50.3% in 1988, depreciated to 10.0% in 2019 and continues to fall even further" (Kamakura 2022: 265). Chinese dominance of the mining and processing of rare earths and critical materials used in batteries, wind turbines, and many electronics products aroused particular unease in Japan and the United States (Daigle and DeCarlo 2021, Leng et al. 2021).

It is true that even as Japan lost ground in the assembly of many final products, it retained significant skills and dominant global market shares in high-end parts and materials used in many valuable products, including semiconductors, batteries, and small electric motors. Yet, even in many of these specialized, high-skill markets, Japanese companies lost ground, while firms from China, South Korea, and Taiwan made inroads (Thorbecke 2019, METI 2022a). In the heady days of the financial bubble of the late 1980s, Japanese firms seemed to be on an inexorable trajectory to become increasingly international, dynamic, and independent of government (Callon 1995). Three decades later, they were indeed more globalized, but appeared far more hesitant and vulnerable.

Continuities in METI's Industrial Policy

Amid a renewed and intensified sense of vulnerability, it became clear that despite all the admittedly significant changes in the political and economic environment, some major continuities characterized government–business relations and the tradition of protecting and promoting Japanese firms. Where once it appeared that METI would abandon its traditional practice of periodically issuing "industrial visions" to guide the development of the Japanese economy (Odaka 2013), in the 2010s, the ministry resumed publication of visions both for the economy as a whole and for individual industries such as semiconductors, textiles, steel, and chemicals.

The METI's share of the government budget remained surprisingly stable, despite the ever-increasing expenditures on pensions and health care required to meet Japan's aging society. The ministry's headcount also remained surprisingly constant, in part reflecting a big increase in staffing for the Japan Patent Office. *Shingikai* deliberation councils continued to operate much as in previous decades, though the "administrative reform" movement of the 1990s and early 2000s did succeed in diluting the influence of vested interests in favor of independent experts and academics, including far more female members (Noble 2002).

Lying behind this continuity in the policy machinery was the nearly unbroken dominance of the pro-business LDP. To be sure, the Democratic Party of Japan (DPJ) managed to capture the cabinet in 2009, in part by running on a campaign promising to replace bureaucratic rule with political leadership. The DPJ soon lost momentum, however, suffering a stinging defeat in the summer 2010 Upper House elections and losing control of the cabinet in 2012. The DPJ soon dissolved and a decade later the LDP was more dominant than ever. Where once Japan was noted for having a "one-and-a-half party system" focused on the LDP and the Japan Socialist Party (then for a brief period the DPJ), it came to resemble Snow White and the seven dwarfs (Noble 2016).

A more lasting challenge came from the centralization of political authority. Increasingly, the Cabinet Secretariat and the Prime Minister's Office initiated and coordinated important policies. Yet they did not do so alone. Much of the expanded staff of the Cabinet Secretariat consisted of officials seconded from the ministries. The METI was so successful in forwarding its staff and proposals that during Prime Minister Abe's long tenure, journalists routinely spoke of the "Abe-METI cabinet" (Shimizu 2016).

Yet, if METI proved surprisingly nimble in charting a path for industrial policy in a political environment increasingly directed by the prime minister and the cabinet, making that policy efficient and effective proved to be exceedingly difficult, as the gap between responsibilities and policy tools widened. Rather than helping rising firms achieve international success, the ministry often found itself bailing out struggling companies. The METI's own policies displayed an uneasy and ever-shifting balance between promoting dynamism and efficiency via "horizontal" policies and using industrial policy interventions into important industries to maintain stability and protect accumulated skills amidst increasing vulnerability.

Despite strains and disappointments, industrial policy did not disappear. Rather, it expanded in two key areas not easily amenable to liberalization and simple reliance on the market: Energy and technology related to national defense. Japan had been reliant on imported energy for decades. The preferred solution of METI and the LDP was to promote nuclear power, which they did with considerable success. The earthquake and tsunami that overwhelmed the Fukushima nuclear power plant in 2011, however, led to a shutdown of all of Japan's nuclear reactors. Many reactors never restarted and the others were slow to return to service. In the interim, Japan was forced to rely on fossil fuel plants that wreaked havoc on the country's commitments to reduce emissions of pollutants and global warming gases. Japan also lagged in development of renewable energy. Once a leader in solar power, Japan struggled to compete with low-cost production from China. Advances in technology for offshore wind power opened up new possibilities, but Japan found itself far behind Europe, the United States, and even China.

A second major area was protecting and promoting technology and skills with important implications for national security. As with energy, this was not a new goal, but it became more pressing as Japan's sense of vulnerability increased. As concerns grew that Japanese firms were losing ground to cheaper, faster, less scrupulous neighbors, particularly China, the government attempted to preserve Japan's technological advantage by preventing outflows of technology and skill. Here again, however, policymakers frequently found themselves seeking to resuscitate declining industries. The government also sought to promote exports of Japanese technology to further diplomatic and security goals, including competing with China's Belt and Road initiative. Particularly after the COVID-19 pandemic and Russia's invasion of Ukraine highlighted the vulnerability of global value chains, in which China played an outsize part, the Japanese government sought to encourage domestic firms to move production to third countries or ideally back to Japan. It encouraged research and development and began to offer major subsidies for crucial industries, especially semiconductors.

Rising National Security Threats amidst Continued Economic Reliance on China

Increasing tensions in Japan's geopolitical environment greatly accentuated the sense of vulnerability. In 1998, North Korea launched the Taepodong-1 medium-range ballistic missile, which flew over Japan before landing in the Pacific Ocean east of Japan. In 2006, North Korea carried out its first nuclear blast test. China posed an even bigger and more all-encompassing threat. China tested its first nuclear weapon in 1964 and launched its first satellite in 1970, but through the 1980s defense spending remained limited. After China joined the WTO in 2001, however, China's economic growth accelerated and by 2006 defense spending in China surpassed that of Japan. While Japanese military spending stagnated, by 2021 Chinese military spending reached $250 billion, outpacing Japanese military expenditures by a factor of five and ranking second only to those of the United States (SIPRI).

Even more threatening were China's aggressive actions in East Asia. In 2005, anti-Japanese demonstrations broke out in several Chinese cities protesting visits by Japanese leaders to Yasukuni Shrine. In 2010, a Chinese fishing vessel collided with a Japanese Coast Guard patrol boat near the disputed Senkaku/ Diaoyu Islands occupied by Japan. Two years later, amidst rising political tensions in both Japan and China, the Japanese government nationalized the Senkaku Islands, sparking anti-Japan demonstrations across China and increasing intrusions into Japanese-claimed waters by Chinese fishing boats and government vessels. Tensions also rose over gas fields straddling the boundary line separating the two countries in the East China Sea and over China's expansive "nine-dash line" claiming almost all of the South China Sea, even after a judgment by an international tribunal rejected China's historically based territorial claims.

Nor were the threats posed by the "rise of China" limited to military affairs. Around the time of the Beijing Olympics in 2008, economic growth peaked at over 10 percent a year and China began to produce and export more sophisticated products. At the same time, the global financial crisis engulfed the United States and Europe, and concerns in the United States about China's industrial espionage, cyberattacks, and infringement of intellectual property rights spiraled (see, for example, Hannas et al. 2013). The Federal Bureau of Investigation (FBI) claimed that where American companies practiced "development by innovation," Chinese business practices were based on "development by theft, reproduction, and commercialization" (FBI 2019: 2). By 2020, the director of the FBI proclaimed that the American people were the victims of "Chinese theft on a scale so massive that it represents one of the largest transfers of wealth in human history" (Wray 2020).

These heated contentions were soon picked up in Japan, which national security officials lamented was so lacking in defenses that it constituted "heaven for [Chinese] spies" (Kitamura and Oyabu 2022). Policy discussions in Japan were, if anything, even more stark than in the United States. They rarely if ever acknowledged that many of the measures adopted by China to advance its technology were common and legal, that many of the countermeasures suggested in the United States would themselves violate the tenets of the WTO, and that many of the prosecutions of supposed Chinese spies in the United States had proved dreadfully misguided and even counterproductive (Guo et al. 2021, Bateman 2022). The palpable sense of vulnerability and the desire to close ranks with the United States completely dominated policy discussions.

Yet at the same time Japan relied much more heavily on economic interactions with China than the United States did. In 2021, China supplied almost a quarter of Japan's imports, and together with Hong Kong absorbed over 26 percent of Japanese exports (JETRO). A range of Japanese industries, including automobiles, electronics, machinery, and textiles, also depended on China as a crucial production base supplying the Chinese and world markets. Tensions with China, or between China and the United States, could deal a serious blow to the Japanese economy. Reducing economic reliance on China might be a desirable long-term goal, but it could be accomplished only gradually and with determination and care.

Economic Security

The concepts of economic security (経済安全保障) and supply chain vulnerability first rose to prominence when China allegedly restricted exports of rare earths to Japan in the aftermath of the 2010 Senkaku boat collision incident (Evenett and Fritz 2023), then heated up in 2017–18 when the Trump administration put increasing pressure on American, European, and Japanese companies not to supply semiconductors and other crucial inputs to the Chinese telecommunications giant Huawei. Trump then levied stiff tariffs on an array of imports from China, inspiring countermeasures from China. The outbreak of the COVID-19 pandemic in 2020 raised further concerns about the dependence of the Japanese medical system on imports, not least from China. In response, former METI minister Amari Akira and other LDP heavyweights pushed the Japanese government to establish an "economic section" (経済班) within the National Security Council in 2020 and to begin drafting an economic security promotion bill (NHK October 21, 2020). The year 2020 marked a watershed in Japanese industrial policy.

In mid-2021, Washington's new Biden administration published a 250-page "100-day review" on how to build resilient supply chains and reinvigorate domestic manufacturing (The White House 2021). Spurred by the growing technology "trade war" between China and the United States, the resulting Japanese bill comprised four elements (Cabinet Secretariat 2022a):

1. Investigate and support the domestic production of critical products and materials such as semiconductors, batteries, and pharmaceuticals.
2. Secure the safety of vital infrastructure, including nuclear power plants, electricity grids, and financial and telecommunications networks.
3. Promote research and development in crucial new technologies such as artificial intelligence.
4. Identify and prevent publication of patents with important national security implications, compensating the inventing firms for any lost royalties.

The bill incorporated both carrots, in the form of subsidies, and sticks, including fines and prison sentences of up to two years. Businesses welcomed the prospect of government support, but Keidanren, many firms, and opposition parties expressed uneasiness at the breadth of coverage and vagueness of the draft bill, which left almost all specifics, such as the identity of materials and industries to be promoted, to be determined by ministerial ordinance (Nikkei, February 26, 2022: 5). However, continuing tensions between the United States and China, and Russia's invasion of Ukraine heightened concerns about dependence on global supply chains. A broad cross-party coalition passed the bill into law in May 2022, with only minor revisions and the inclusion of a supplementary resolution piously calling on the government to 'respect the autonomy of enterprise activities' (*Asahi*, May 12, 2022: 1, 2) (Cabinet Secretariat 2022a). The concept of economic security thus became enshrined in Japanese law and politics and increasingly guided the implementation of industrial policy.

If Japanese industrial policy, particularly vertical policy to protect and promote specific industries, became steadily less intrusive after the 1980s, a good deal of continuity remained. With the adoption of economic security as a guiding principle in 2020, however, both the policy environment and the policy tool kit experienced a fundamental transformation. From the 1960s through the 2010s the global economy grew steadily more open and globalized, but a backlash against market-oriented "neo-liberal" policies, and the growing inequality and instability for which they were blamed, gradually spread, reaching a high point with the election of the explicitly protectionist Trump administration in the United States, which raised tariffs sharply and deliberately hobbled the World Trade Organization (WTO). Once a large and rising economy, Japan steadily lost ground not only to China and South Korea but also to the United States. Where Japanese exports seemed to threaten American economic dominance in the 1980s and 1990s, by 2020 the United States viewed Japan as a like-minded and unthreatening alternative to relying on China for vital inputs to supply chains. Security relations also transformed. Japan had long passively hosted American military bases in return for security guarantees, but increasingly the two countries agreed that Japan should play a more active role in providing military forces, defense technology, and an ever-expanding list of dual use products, particularly semiconductors. The range of policy tools became narrower but more emphatic. Policy loans, tariffs, restrictions on foreign capital, and tax breaks all continued to fade, while direct subsidies from the budget suddenly multiplied. "Economic security" became the crucial concept animating and justifying Japan's new industrial policy.

2 Institutional Continuity but Fewer Tools – until 2020

Despite major changes in the political, economic, and administrative environment outlined in Section 1 that reduced the policy tools available to the Japanese government to promote specific industries, much of the mechanism of industrial

policy, including ministerial organization, personnel structure, budgetary allocations, and public–private consultation systems, remained in place. Policymakers
concentrated more on "horizontal" measures to enhance the flexibility, efficiency,
and innovative capacity of the whole economy, such as reforming corporate
governance, strengthening protection of intellectual property, and promoting
start-up companies, though "vertical" industrial policy did not disappear, and
the energy sector remained an abiding concern. After 2020, however, rapidly
increasing concerns about macroeconomic stability and economic security led to
the compilation of huge supplementary budgets that funded numerous programs
to promote energy and strategic industrial technology.

Organization

Reorganization of central ministries and agencies in 2001 gave METI a new
name – Ministry of *Economy*, Trade and Industry – and enhanced its jurisdiction
and responsibilities (Elder 2003). The ministry absorbed most of the policy
research functions of the old Economic Planning Agency, which previously had
been under the wing of the Ministry of Finance. The reorganization also created
a high-profile Research Institute of Economy, Trade and Industry (RIETI), led
initially by presidents with long experience at prestigious American universities
and staffed by about sixty full-time researchers who received high salaries but
pointedly did not enjoy civil service status. A diverse group of part-time fellows
from universities, government agencies and ministries, and other organizations
included many of Japan's most prominent economists.

As part of its drive to enhance the position of Japanese firms in the
international political economy, METI strengthened the protection of intellectual
property rights, primarily by greatly expanding the Japan Patent Office (JPO).
Established in 1885, soon after the Meiji Restoration, by 2020 it boasted a budget
of over a billion dollars, supported by fees, and a staff of over 2,800 (Ministry of
Finance Budget Bureau 2022: 373, 381). Along with its counterparts in the United
States and Europe, the JPO gained recognition as one of the world's three premier
patent authorities.

METI re-organized the National Institute of Advanced Industrial Science and
Technology (AIST), a "national research and development corporation" whose
connection to METI and its predecessors dated back to 1882. A collection of
research institutes mostly headquartered in the "science city" of Tsukuba, just
north of Tokyo, by 2020 AIST employed around 3,000 researchers and admin-
istrators, supported by 1,500 technical staff, and a budget of nearly $1 billion
(AIST 2020).

Similarly, METI continued to support the closely affiliated Japan External Trade Organization (JETRO), with a staff of around 1,900, one-third of whom were deployed overseas. In 1998 it merged with the Institute of the Developing Economies (IDE), still known in Japanese as the Asian Economy Research Institute. In 2003 JETRO – along with many other governmental entities, including national universities – was re-organized as an independent administrative corporation but remained dependent on METI for funding, staffing, and leadership.

METI continued to place particular emphasis on energy and related technologies. In the summer of 1973, as energy imports surged and the Middle East careened toward the first oil crisis, METI transformed its coal mining and public enterprises sections into the Agency for Natural Resources and Energy (ANRE), which became well-known for creating the Sunshine and Moonlight Projects to promote the development of renewable energy and energy conservation.

In 1980, following the second oil crisis, METI established the New Energy and Industrial Technology Development Organization (NEDO). Originally focused on energy, in 1988 its ambit expanded to include industrial technology. In 2003, it became a "national research and development agency," still under the jurisdiction of METI. As of 2022, it had a staff of about 1,400 and a budget of a little over US$1 billion, plus five large "publicly solicited research and development projects" (NEDO).

At the same time, METI continued to display a practical, local orientation. METI itself possessed eight regional industrial diffusion offices around the country to support local firms, such as manufacturers of automotive parts, and maintained close connections with industrial technology centers located in almost every one of Japan's forty-seven prefectures.

As Elder (2003) noted, after the re-organization of 2001, the number of industry-specific (vertical) divisions (課) shrank, implying a decreasing emphasis on industrial policy in favor of "horizontal" or functional policies affecting all industries, such as promotion of venture capital or revision of the commercial code. Yet the decline in vertical divisions dated back to the 1970s (Odaka 2013) and was far from complete. As of the early 2020s, METI's Manufacturing Industries Bureau included seven divisions responsible for specific industries: aerospace and defense, industrial machinery, automobiles, metals, chemicals, materials, and "lifestyle products." Many other industry-specific divisions fell under the Commerce and Information Policy Bureau, including information technology, media and contents, bio-industry, distribution, retail industries, and many energy-related divisions.

Personnel

As with organizational structure, the personnel system responsible for implementing industrial policy, like the Japanese economy as a whole, is a little looser and more diverse than in previous decades, but it still displays considerable continuity (cf. Vogel 2021). Schaede and Shimizu (2022) and many Japanese journalists note that the relative popularity and prestige of careers in the central government ministries have declined in recent years: from 2000 to 2022, the number of applicants to the higher civil-service examination decreased by more than half, the dominance of the most demanding and prestigious universities, led by the University of Tokyo and Kyoto University, declined, and an increasing number of elite or "career" bureaucrats abandoned the civil service early in their careers (Ozawa 2019, National Personnel Authority 2021). That is true. Elite bureaucrats in Japan worked grueling hours, particularly when the Diet was in session and government officials had to draft answers for their ministers to deploy in parliamentary question time. Government salaries also had a hard time competing with those of financial and technology firms, or leading business consultancies. The tight labor market of the preceding decade only intensified these contrasts.

Yet as of 2021, applicants to the elite-track civil service exam (国家公務員総合職試験, before 2012 known as 1種試験) still outnumbered available positions by nearly 8 to 1 (National Personnel Authority 2021), and METI still ranked near the top in perceived power and morale. A study by a cram school preparing candidates for the civil service examination found that METI was one of four "super ministries" that were hardest to test into, along with the Ministry of Finance, Ministry of Internal Affairs and Communications, and the National Police Agency (Koumuin-senmon.com). According to a massive survey of employees by a recruiting agency, METI ranked in the top 2 percent of the 167,850 public and private employers covered. Despite demanding the longest overtime hours, its overall evaluation score of 3.58 and morale score of 3.74 were by far the highest of any government ministry or agency except the Japan Patent Office, itself part of METI (Openwork).

Entry tests include not only a difficult written examination but also a follow-up round of interviews at the ministry. The interview portion of the exam had gained prominence in recent years, partly to put more emphasis on recruiting candidates with a positive and cooperative attitude (Ozawa 2019), and partly to increase the proportion of women, who now accounted for about 35 percent of new elite-track recruits for the ministries as a whole and about 29 percent at METI (Noble 2019, Cabinet Secretariat Personnel Division 2022). Enhanced emphasis on interviews and recruiting women may also help account for the decline in hiring from the most elite universities, whose graduates tended to excel in written examinations and were overwhelmingly male.

After recruitment, career patterns at METI still mostly followed a familiar course. New hires generally entered METI immediately after graduating from university or, in about one-third of cases, from graduate or professional school, forming an annual cohort of about fifty members. Regular rotation every two or three years gave members an opportunity to work at a variety of jobs within the ministry. Occasionally they were seconded for two or three years to graduate or professional schools (often abroad); regional offices; agencies or associations affiliated with METI; Japanese embassies or consulates abroad; the cabinet office; or even other ministries, but responsibility for evaluating and guiding their career progression remained with the home ministry. That is, METI remained one of a number of ministerial silos.

After ten years or so, the most promising members were increasingly appointed to the most responsible and demanding posts. When one of the most outstanding members was finally appointed at the age of sixty or so to a two or three-year term as administrative vice minister (the highest position open to a career official, as opposed to a politician), all the other members of the same age or older retired from the ministry and sought "post-retirement" positions outside the ministry. This was the (in)famous practice of *amakudari*, or "descent from heaven." For the first two years after retirement, former officials had to seek permission from the National Personnel Authority to accept employment in areas covered by the last five years of their work in the ministry.

Popular images of *amakudari* have evolved through roughly three stages. During the rapid growth period, the typical case of *amakudari* was seen as a graduate of the law faculty of the University of Tokyo who passed the upper civil-service exam, served in a ministry until about age sixty, then accepted a highly paid and often undemanding position, arranged by the ministry's personnel section, as director or high-level executive of a private-sector firm in his former ministry's area of jurisdiction. In the case of MITI, that might mean employment at an electric power utility, general trading company, or major manufacturer. The company acquired information, connections, access to the ministries, and gratitude (or at least credit) for having helped the ministry, while the former officials received cushy and lucrative jobs and generous retirement payments to make up for those years of grueling overtime and modest salaries.

As the economy liberalized, growth slowed, and cries mounted for reform of *amakudari* and the bureaucracy as a whole, re-employment at corporations declined somewhat and attention shifted to the increasing number of former bureaucrats who found post-ministry employment at one of the myriad semi-public organizations or nonprofit companies affiliated with the ministry (Nakano 2009). Indeed, critics charged that many of these organizations had been established specifically to provide convenient parking spots for ex-bureaucrats.

Finally, in the decades after re-organization of the central ministries, attention shifted to the increasing number of ex-bureaucrats, particularly from METI, who departed early to take up active positions in start-up companies, high-tech firms, consultancies, and foreign companies, where their major appeal was substantive expertise rather than insider information and government contacts.

How accurate are these popular impressions of the changing face of *amakudari*? While the available data, based on mandatory reports filed with the National Personnel Authority (NPA), provide evidence of all three patterns, "type two" re-employment with the semi-public sector looms largest. Of the fifty METI officials who filed reports with the NPA in the first ten months of 2021, fewer than 30 percent took positions with private companies, while the others moved to associations, universities, government entities, or self-employment. Only ten were hired as board members (専務理事 or 常務理事), none of them at for-profit companies; only two were company directors (取締役). As at most ministries, the large majority of workers departed in their fifties. "Type three" early departures were indeed somewhat more common at METI than at other ministries: five of the early leavers – all lawyers–were in their twenties and thirties, while one information security specialist was in his forties (compiled by author from entries at Amakudari-log). In addition, some former officials assumed unrelated positions immediately after retiring from METI, then switched to private-sector jobs related to their areas of specialization after the mandatory two-year cooling-off period.

If we restrict our attention to top ministry officials, the connection with the private sector remained clearer. Until the early 1990s, former administrative vice ministers of MITI typically became company directors in mainline industries such as steel, petroleum, and electric power. After that, some former AVMs took positions in the semi-public sector. In the decade after Abe Shinzo became prime minister in 2011, former heads of the Agency for Natural Resources and Energy (ANRE) took positions as company directors at Mitsubishi Electric, Fujitsu, and the giant trading house Marubeni, as well as the Japanese government's overseas petroleum exploration and production company INPEX.

In sum, *amakudari* second careers are still the norm. Some top officials still assume traditional "type 1" company director positions at mainstream firms under METI's jurisdiction, and a few young officials do jump ship early to take "type 3" jobs in law or technology. However, the large majority of career officials retire in their late fifties to take relatively modest "type 2" positions in the public or semi-public realm. The scope of the METI network is still impressively broad and thick, but direct connections with private firms via *amakudari* have declined somewhat.

Industrial Visions

During the rapid growth period, METI gained fame for periodically issuing "visions" of the future of Japanese industry. Foreseeing the future was not so difficult when Japan was still in catch-up mode and could look to North America and Europe for a glimpse of things to come, and the process of formulating industrial visions in conjunction with the private sector helped generate information and coordinate expectations and investments among Japanese firms (Okuno-Fujiwara 1988). By the 1980s and 1990s, however, Japanese firms had reached the global technology frontier in most areas (though as noted in the previous section, they sometimes fell back again as foreign firms moved more quickly into new areas). Facing a cloudy future and criticized by foreign partners for allegedly unfair trade and industrial policies, METI and affiliated scholars piously averred that the era of industrial visions had passed (Odaka 2013: 19, 573).

Yet in 2010, METI's premier public–private consultation committee, the Industrial Structure Council, released another grand vision of industrial structure. The vision called for changes in industrial structure, business models, employment, and the role of government. The report identified five strategic sectors: (1) Infrastructure-related systems export; (2) environment and energy problem-solving industries, such as smart grids and next-generation vehicles; (3) medical, nursing, and childcare services; (4) cultural industries including fashion, contents, food, and tourism; and (5) frontier fields like robotics and aerospace (METI 2010).

In 2017, after commissioning a 430-page background report by the Boston Consulting Group, the ministry released an even grander vision of a new industrial structure. Building on a concept originating in Germany and propagated by the World Economic Forum of a "Fourth Industrial Revolution" and Japan's own concept of "Society 5.0" (METI 2017),

> The New Industrial Structure Vision leverages Japan's strengths to realize an active and comfortable Society 5.0. These strengths include Japan's capacity to gather and use data, its pioneering use of technology to create innovative products, and its drive to offer solutions to developing social

issues. METI has identified how each of these strengths can be used to solve problems in the fields of Mobility, Supply Chains, Healthcare, and Lifestyle.

"Breakthrough projects" in each field included establishing a Center of Excellence to integrate artificial intelligence with manufacturing technologies and creating a new, integrated system of personal health records.

In 2020, METI issued a more focused "vision" specifically for industrial technology, describing how Society 5.0 could be achieved by developing intellectual capital and the "intelligence of things," including integration of software, robotics, and sensing. The report called on Japanese to be more open, innovative, individualistic, entrepreneurial, and international – but also reiterated the importance of industrial competitiveness, economic security, energy, and the development of flexible, resilient supply chains (METI 2020: 8–13). Industries of special interest included next-generation computing, bio-tech, and energy and the environment. Similar, if more focused, reports covered such fields as materials, textiles, and next-generation automobiles.

In short, METI has not abandoned mapping the future. If the ministry's visions of industrial structure and industrial technology sometimes appear sprawling and abstract, they display a consistent concern for two fields with important implications for national security: the impact of semiconductors and advanced computing, and the energy-CO_2 nexus.

Budgets

An examination of the budgetary resources supporting METI's industrial policy also reveals more continuity than change and a recurrent concern for technology and energy. Surprisingly, given the ever-increasing share of the budget dedicated to servicing the national debt and defraying the cost of healthcare and pensions for an aging population, METI commanded a modest but relatively constant share of the national budget over the half century from 1970 to 2020.

The METI budget itself, however, has been far from static or incremental. Instead, it reveals clear changes in emphasis. Most obviously, after the oil shocks of the 1970s, energy emerged as the most important focus of the budget, while the resources devoted to small- and medium-sized enterprises slowly but surely drifted down. In contrast, despite the consistent rhetorical attention paid to technology, the funding devoted to its promotion was surprisingly volatile, and actually declined over the course of the 2010s.

METI Budgets 1970–2022
(initial General Account budgets, in thousand yen)

Year/ Area	TOTAL Government	METI	METI share	SME	SME/ METI	S&T	S&T/ METI	Energy	Energy/ METI
1970	7,949,764,116	97,260,112	1.2%	37,151,120	38.2%	18,209,616	18.7%	NA	NA
1980	42,588,843,011	646,941,560	1.5%	179,897,451	27.8%	61,133,714	9.4%	264,383,654	40.9%
1990	66,236,790,811	726,341,901	1.1%	135,234,842	18.6%	55,580,046	7.6%	390,316,565	53.7%
2000	84,987,053,259	602,669,127	0.7%	132,533,370	22.0%	81,209,300	13.5%	196,870,611	32.7%
2010	92,299,192,619	992,166,609	1.1%	125,468,888	12.6%	131,059,198	13.2%	581,200,000	58.6%
2020	102,657,971,326	1,243,458,715	1.2%	114,099,404	9.2%	113,298,911	9.1%	607,565,000	48.9%
2022	107,596,424,588	902,389,830	0.8%	109,473,506	12.1%	110,395,667	12.2%	551,160,000	61.1%

SME: Small- and medium-sized enterprises

S&T: Science and technology

Source: Compiled by the author from (Ministry of Finance Budget Bureau various years)

METI's budget for 2020 was consistent with these broad trends but provided more detail. The budget was notable for the heavy weight of energy-related expenditures and the frequent invocations of "economic security" and the need to strengthen the resilience and toughness (強靭化) of Japan's economy and infrastructure. The many programs for small- and medium-sized enterprises were described in loving detail, but mostly restrained in size. Similarly, the budget failed to showcase any big national projects but listed many small programs for technology development. These were mostly modest in size and practical in orientation, involving provision of information, coordination, industrial standards, experiments, and verification tests.

Policy Priorities in METI's 2020 Budget
(Note: the average exchange rate in 2020 was 1 USD = ¥107)

I. Reconstruct Fukushima: ¥101 billion
 – ¥47 billion for nuclear-related damages and decommissioning of nuclear reactors.
II. Respond to the digital economy: ¥50 billion
 – ¥5 billion for automated driving and "mobility as a service"
 – ¥6.7 billion for artificial intelligence and critical robotic technology development, including experiments, verification, and transmission of tacit knowledge
 – ¥3 billion for construction of digital platforms for e-government
III. Promote free and fair trade and devise global countermeasures for climate change: ¥69 billion
 – ¥25 billion contribution to JETRO
 – ¥1.6 billion for technologies to promote economic resilience and national security
 – ¥1.7 billion for feasibility studies for development of "high-quality infrastructure" overseas
IV. Develop a foundation for a new growth model: ¥143 billion
 – ¥6 billion to cultivate researchers and promote "J-Startup" companies
 – ¥80 billion for R&D and social implementation of Society 5.0, including subsidies for electric and hybrid vehicles; development of semiconductors for artificial intelligence; and measures to support the growth of small- and medium-sized companies and strengthen the earning power of regions
V. Strengthen the economic security of Japan's energy base: ¥748 billion
 – ¥305 billion for energy transition and de-carbonization, including R&D for hydrogen fuel cells, carbon recycling, and high-efficiency gas turbines

(cont.)

    – ¥443 billion to explore domestic oil and gas fields and develop technology to process methane hydrate

VI. Implement measures to offset the increase in the consumption tax: ¥2,753

    – Consumer rebates for "cashless" transactions at small- and medium-sized enterprises

VII. Strengthen the national infrastructure against natural disasters: ¥34 billion

---

Source: Compiled by author from 経済産業省関係令和 2 年度当初予算の概要 (Overview of METI-related items in the initial 2020 budget). https://www.meti.go.jp/main/yosan/yosan_fy2020/pdf/keisanshoyosan2.pdf

This picture of relative budgetary stability came to an abrupt halt in the latter part of 2020. Most years, the government compiled one or two supplementary budgets equivalent to less than 5 percent of the general account budget to cope with natural disasters and other miscellaneous shocks. However, in 2020, as the pandemic shut down much of the country's economic activity and the United States pressured Japan to spend more on national security, the government responded with an unprecedented supplementary budget more than an order of magnitude larger, allocating $682 billion after a general account budget of $962 billion. Succeeding supplementary budgets shrank somewhat, but still equaled about a third of the general account budget in 2021 and 2022, and one-tenth in 2023 (Ministry of Finance).

As in the United States and other countries, most of this massive spending was designed to prop up employment and consumption, but it also allowed for a major increase in spending on energy and industrial technology. The second supplementary budget of 2022 alone allocated roughly $10 billion to support a welter of consortia and cooperative efforts to promote the semiconductor industry. And while these were in principle one-off expenditures, the second supplementary budget included an unprecedented and controversial $68 billion to create various endowment funds (基金) that could be drawn upon in subsequent years (*Asahi* November 22, 2022).

Policy Tools: Reduced

In contrast to the relatively high degree of continuity observable in METI's organization, personnel, visions, and budgets, an examination of policy tools available to influence the decisions of the private sector reveals a steep decline – until the sharp turn toward national economic security policy beginning in 2020.

As noted in Section 1, controls over foreign exchange largely disappeared decades ago. Barriers against imports and foreign investment sharply declined in the 1980s and 1990s, both in response to pressure from the United States and other allies and as part of Japan's move to expand outward direct foreign investment and build elaborate regional and global production networks. Rather than protecting the domestic market with tariffs, METI's trade policy increasingly focused on promoting bilateral, regional, and global trade and investment agreements.

Tax breaks also declined in significance. Corporate tax rates were cut sharply in the late 1990s and again in the 2010s under Abe, decreasing the value of tax breaks that METI could wangle out of the Ministry of Finance.

The role of policy finance, always more limited in Japan than in South Korea, Taiwan, or China, shrank further. The Fiscal Investment and Loan Program, often called the "second budget," contracted (Park 2011). Public-sector banks, such as the Development Bank of Japan and Shoko Chukin Bank, were never very strategic (Calder 1993) and always more under the influence of MOF than of MITI/METI. Periodic scandals and complaints that public banks were crowding out private sector financial institutions led to some privatization and mergers of government-related banks and to the emergence of a Financial Services Agency independent of the Ministry of Finance.

Even more important was the change in the private sector financial system. The Long-term Bank Act of 1952 had authorized a small group of banks led by the Industrial Bank of Japan (IBJ) to provide long-term corporate lending. These long-term banks enjoyed a privileged regulatory position and close relations with METI and MOF during the rapid growth period. However, massive changes in the economic environment from the early 1990s, particularly the collapse in interest rates after the bursting of the financial bubble, rendered them obsolete. The Long-term Credit Bank became dependent on risky real estate lending, was nationalized in 1998, and then sold off to foreign investors and renamed Shinsei ("New Life") Bank in 2000. Similarly, Nippon Credit Bank collapsed in 1998, was nationalized, sold off, and equally optimistically renamed Aozora ("Blue Sky") in 2001, while IBJ merged into Mizuho, one of three new megabanks emerging from the collapse of the financial bubble.

Over the next decade and particularly after 2012, corporate finances gradually improved. Companies were increasingly able to fund their own investments through retained earnings and corporate bonds. Returns on equity, though improved, continued to trail those of the United States, the United Kingdom, and Europe (BlackRock 2024), but few large Japanese companies depended upon policy financing mediated by METI.

The ministry's organization, staffing, funding, and consultative networks remained surprisingly robust, but the policy tools with which to elicit cooperation from private firms declined sharply until the early 2020s and the advent of giant supplemental budgets aiming to shore up economic security.

3 Political Relations: Old Constituents, New Boss

Industrial policy is the product of the interaction between pilot agencies and external actors, particularly the business community and the political leadership. Policy is neither unilaterally imposed by a dominant bureaucracy nor neatly captured by big business firms, industry associations, and peak lobbying groups, but reflects a balance of forces, in which each group can exert some influence and block the more extreme proposals of the others. Samuels (1987) usefully referred to this balance as a politics of "reciprocal consent." METI and other bureaucracies "adjust interests" and draft policy in consultation with business and the ruling party; business provides investment and employment, including reemployment of former ministry officials, along with campaign contributions to politicians; while politicians lobby for specific policies in return for ensuring that bills and budgets pass the Diet. Politicians look after small- and medium-sized firms and specific geographic regions, and policy tends to favor existing interests over nascent economic forces. Since the early 1960s, "creative destruction" has been decidedly limited (Katz 2023).

Trends in external relations are largely similar to those seen in Section 2 concerning METI's internal operations: the fundamental framework of industrial policy remained largely intact, but from the 1990s relations with business became somewhat more distant and formal, while the key connection to the LDP shifted from business-oriented backbenchers and mid-level leaders of "policy tribes" to the prime minister, cabinet, and top party executives.

Partly as a result, the balance between "horizontal" policies affecting all industries, and "vertical" industrial policies focused on specific industries, shifted in the direction of the former until 2020, when the top leadership pushed to the forefront the strategic selection of industries and technologies seen as vital to national security.

Peak Business Federations

Today, Japan has three major business federations, of which the most important is Keidanren. Founded in the Meiji period, the Japan Chamber of Commerce and Industry (JCCI 日本商工会議所, 日商) is an alliance of 515 local chambers of commerce. It represents mainly small firms, but traditionally it has been led by a big business executive (since 2013, the head of Nippon Steel). As of 2022, a former METI official had been on the JCCI's board of directors since 2013. Small firms are a vital political constituency of the LDP, but the JCCI is not terribly important in setting national policy, though local chambers can play some role in implementation.

As its name suggests, the Japan Association of Corporate Executives (Keizai Doyukai 経済同友会) is comprised not of firms or associations but of individual business executives. Founded in 1946 by young executives who had escaped the Occupation purge, by the 2020s it had a membership of about 1,500 and a staff of 72. For at least two decades, no METI officials reported taking up employment there. Compared to Keidanren, Keizai Doyukai is more individualistic, has greater representation of women and foreign firms, and more consistently espouses a market-oriented "neo-liberal" agenda. Its members played a crucial role in the de-regulatory movement under Prime Minister Koizumi Junichiro and proved more open to dialogue with the DPJ cabinet of the early 2010s. Not surprisingly, it has not been a major proponent of industrial policy.

As of April 1, 2022, the membership of Japan's premier business association, Japan Business Federation or Keidanren (日本経済団体連合会), was comprised of 1,494 firms and 155 associations, including 47 regional groupings. It had a formidable staff of 228 and its own think tank, the 21st Century Public Policy Institute, established in 1997. Particularly under Prime Ministers Koizumi Junichiro (2001–06) and Abe Shinzo (2006–07; 2012–20), Keidanren Chairs played leading roles in deliberative committees such as the influential Council on Economic and Fiscal Policy.

Most of Keidanren's member firms were large, established industrial companies, though in recent years there has been some move away from manufacturing: as of 2022, eight of the nineteen vice chairs represented financial or general trading firms, including the largest securities firm and Japan's three mega banks (Keidanren). Reflecting the low level of inward foreign direct investment, Keidanren's member firms were overwhelmingly headquartered in Japan, though many had significant levels of foreign stock ownership.

Direct METI influence has declined: Keidanren's third chair (Uemura Kogoro) served in METI's predecessor and in wartime economic planning posts and then headed Keidanren's secretariat before ascending to the federation's top spot from 1968 to 1974, but in recent decades METI officials have not moved to Keidanren.

Before the 1990s, political funding from member firms arranged by Keidanren played a critical role in supporting the LDP and thus indirectly in supporting the conservative regime in which industrial policy flourished. After reforms to the electoral system and campaigning activities law, however, contributions by big businesses shrank relative to the new system of public funding of elections, which accounted for about 2/3 of the LDP's reported income in 2020 (*Mainichi* November 27, 2021). When other parties controlled the cabinet in 1993–94 and 2009–12, Keidanren withdrew from political funding altogether. It resumed organizing business contributions in 2014, but had little to say about industrial policy, limiting itself to issuing annual advisory "policy report cards" that praised the LDP and to a lesser extent its coalition partner Komeito and ignored or denigrated the other parties.

Befitting its size and influence, Keidanren has an elaborate structure, including seventy-odd committees. Some cover economy-wide issues such as taxes, labor, and intellectual property rights, while others tackle cross-industrial problems such as logistics and supply chains. Only a handful focus on specific industries, notably aerospace and defense, agriculture, and tourism. Most committees cover issues quite distant from industry, including population, consumers, social security, crisis management, politics, and foreign affairs, plus two dozen committees devoted to individual foreign countries. Perhaps partly because of the diversity of its membership and policy concerns, Keidanren is less consistently neo-liberal than Keizai Doyukai.

Many recent accounts of Keidanren claim that it has lost effectiveness and political influence (Mori 2014). This is partially true, if only because the Japanese business community has grown more globalized and diverse than during the rapid growth period (and less central to political fundraising). But mostly it is unwarranted nostalgia for the good old days when the chairman of Keidanren was a grand old man hobnobbing with LDP leaders and hailed as "the Prime Minister of the business community." In recent decades, Keidanren leadership has become less personalistic and more routinized (Sasaki 2016). Younger chairs serve regular four-year terms and preside over a much more developed system of interest aggregation and policy deliberation.

In sum, despite some reforms, Keidanren still has a status quo bias and an orientation to heavy industry. It is an important complement to METI in efforts to stimulate the overall economy, but in recent decades it has typically had only an indirect connection to industry policy.

New Challengers to Keidanren?

In recent years, two new federations have emerged that potentially challenge Keidanren's dominant position and policy stances. The first centers on the software industry. After the Fukushima nuclear disaster in 2011, Mikitani Hiroshi, a graduate of Harvard Business School and founder and CEO of e-commerce giant Rakuten, announced that he was resigning from Keidanren to protest its continued support of nuclear power and its reluctance to undertake fundamental reforms to make Japanese companies more competitive. The next year he founded the Japanese Association of New Economy (JANE 新経済連盟, 新経連). A decade later, with Mikitani still serving as representative director, membership had grown to 160 listed firms and about 300 others, including a few based overseas. JANE's thirteen project teams mostly covered the new economy – innovation, fintech, start-ups, and blockchain technology; none focused on individual industries, with the exception of real estate and tourism (JANE). In places, JANE overlaps with Keidanren, for example in concerns for education and immigration policy, but it is much smaller, narrower, and lower profile than Keidanren or Keizai Doyukai, and except for nuclear power, has little to do with industrial policy.

In sharp contrast to the cautious attitude toward global warming of Keidanren and METI, the Japan Climate Initiative (JCI 気候変動イニシアティブ), established by 105 member organizations in 2018, represents an aggressive effort to lobby for de-carbonization. By 2022 it included 526 companies (many of which also belonged to Keidanren, Keizai Doyukai, or JANE), 37 local governments, and 143 other organizations. But despite its smaller size and tighter focus, JCI still has difficulty reaching consensus on specific issues, especially the role of nuclear power. Fewer than half of member companies, local governments, and NGOs (and neither JANE nor the three peak business organizations) signed onto JCI's appeal to the Japanese government to have renewable energy – specifically excluding nuclear power – supply 40–50 percent of Japan's power needs by 2030 (JCI 2022).

Industry Associations

More directly important for industrial policy are associations linking firms in specific industries. Industry or trade associations that devise common positions and lobby government on taxes, labor, and regulation are not limited to Japan, of course, but they are more ubiquitous and better organized than in most other advanced democracies. In Japan's vital automotive industry, for example, all of the major assemblers, such as Toyota and Nissan, belong to the Japan Automobile Manufacturers Association (JAMA), with fourteen members. Most of the larger producers of automotive components belong to the Japan Auto Parts Industries Association (JAPIA), with about 430 members, accounting for only 6 percent of the firms in the industry, but 60 percent of parts output (JAPIA). Other associations represent automotive dealers and importers. Most large firms also belong to one of the peak associations.

Trade associations carry out a myriad of functions, including drafting technical standards, conducting surveys, and implementing industrial testing, verification, and experiments for new products and production processes. Sometimes, particularly in the past, they have formed quasi-cartels (Tilton 1996). Industry associations, led by autos, steel, oil, electronics, and chemicals, remain significant sources of political contributions to the LDP, though their relative importance has declined with the advent of public funding for political parties.

Trade associations are under the legal jurisdiction of specific ministries such as METI and their activities gain some credibility from the tinge of quasi-governmental authority. For example, officials from METI and executives from the automobile industry and the Japan Automobile Manufacturers Association regularly fly to the International Organization for Standardization (ISO) head-quarters in Geneva to present a unified Japanese position on autonomous driving and charging formats for electric vehicles.

METI's presence in industry associations is much more visible than in peak federations such as Keidanren. According to reports filed with the National Personnel Authority, in recent years, former METI officials joined the boards of directors for industry associations ranging from steel, machinery, and aerospace to software and information. They assumed posts as managing directors or chief of the secretariat of associations covering chemicals, electronics, and cameras and image displays. Others served as vice chairpersons for automobiles and chemical fibers (Amakudari-log).

Deliberation Councils (審議会等)

Another crucial connection between industrial policy and the business commu-nity comes in the form of deliberative councils, or *shingikai*. These, too, are not unique to Japan but are unusual in their density and influence. During the rapid growth period, these councils were often portrayed as little more than "fairy cloaks of invisibility" barely covering bureaucratic dominance: "Bureaucrats exercise a large amount of influence over the selection of *shingikai* members, control 'the areas of investigation,' provide the staff and expertise for investi-gation, and draft the reports" (Koh 1989: 207). By the 1990s, Schwartz (1998) characterized them as arenas for neo-pluralist bargaining among interest groups, with the degree of bureaucratic influence varying depending on the breadth and exclusivity of jurisdiction, and (negatively) with the degree of divisibility of the output, since politicians are loath to pass up opportunities to claim credit for distributing valued goods. At about the same time, deliberative councils came in for criticism by advocates of administrative and political reform, who argued that the crucial deliberation over policy should be con-ducted by parties and in the Diet.

The critiques led to a paring back of ministerial councils and a rise in prominence of councils advising the prime minister and cabinet. Academics and women replaced most interest group representatives even in the most prestigious councils – METI's Industrial Structure Council (ISC) and the Ministry of Finance's Fiscal System Council (Kamba 2015). In 2019, METI even went so far as to eliminate industry-based committees from the ISC.

And yet here again change was not as abrupt as it might appear. Much of the action shifted away from formal shingikai and toward less tightly regulated forms. In the case of the automobile industry, for example, METI convened a business-dominated Strategy Council (戦略会議) for the New Automotive Age in 2018–19, followed by an investigative commission (検討会) on the structure of mobility in 2030 and beyond, both of which balanced academics and industry representatives.

Dealing with New Political Masters

After the advent of political administrative reforms in the early 2000s, the political environment surrounding industrial policy grew more volatile and ministers became more independent of their bureaucratic underlings. Once selected without much reference to their experience and shifted every year or two to ensure that each senior LDP politician received an opportunity to serve in the cabinet, ministers relied heavily on the expertise and continuity provided by the career bureaucrats, and often served as little more than cheerleaders for bureaucratic initiatives. After the reforms of the 1990s, increasingly ministers were selected on the basis of qualifications and political influence and brought their own agendas (Pekkanen, Nyblade, and Krauss 2014).

The biggest threat to METI and other ministries came when the Democratic Party of Japan captured the cabinet in 2009. The DPJ challenge to bureaucratic leadership was sharp but short and mostly ineffectual. The DPJ ran on a platform promising political leadership, demonizing the bureaucracy, and threatening *ama-kudari*. It sought to benefit labor and city dwellers and bypassed the Council on Economic and Fiscal Policy, with its heavy business representation. It tried to restructure the budget, threatening particularistic interests supportive of the LDP. But the DPJ never succeeded in creating an alternative policymaking process and lost political momentum in less than a year (Kushida and Lipscy 2013).

The LDP's return to power in 2012 posed new challenges. While METI and industrial policy still operated under the auspices of LDP rule, the influence of LDP factions and mid-level *zoku giin* (policy tribes), many of which, including the "commerce and industry *zoku*," served as vital cheerleaders for ministry initiatives, was largely supplanted by the prime minister's office and cabinet secretariat. Control over high-level bureaucratic appointments and major policy initiatives largely shifted to the cabinet, and ministries competed to have their officials seconded to the prime minister's office and cabinet secretariat.

Fortunately for METI, its members proved unusually adept at making themselves useful to the LDP leadership. As noted in Section 1, under Abe Shinzo, the ministry was so successful at advising the prime minister that journalists took to referring to the "METI cabinet." This was not, however, an institutionalized equilibrium. METI's influence waned under Abe's successor Suga Yoshihide before reaching a balance with the Ministry of Finance under Prime Minister Kishida Fumio, who took the unusual step of appointing the top METI official as his chief political secretary (*Nikkei* October 11, 2021). Even more than in the past, the key to METI's industrial policy lay in the hands of the top LDP leadership.

4 Industrial Policy for Energy

Energy occupies a central place in Japanese industrial policy. Petroleum, gas, electricity, and other sectors of the energy complex are major industries in their own right. Energy, particularly electricity generation, is a major contributor to pollution and global warming. Reliance on energy imports threatens military and economic security.

Yet, energy policy in Japan is puzzling: among the G7 countries, Japan relies most heavily on fossil fuels to generate electricity. The lagging transition to renewables is especially puzzling because Japan has long feared dependence on external energy sources (Graham 2005). From the early 1960s, imports of cheap and abundant oil displaced Japan's dwindling supply of coal, and in the mid-1960s, Japan pioneered large-scale imports of liquefied natural gas (LNG) and began building nuclear power plants. Renewables played little role. One telling exception: the government actively promoted solar power for a brief period when Japanese firms led the world in production technology and manufacturing efficiency, but in recent years even solar has fallen behind (IRENA 2022c: 17–22, REN21 2022).

Even more surprisingly, despite an upswelling of public opposition to nuclear power after the Fukushima meltdown in 2011, and despite remarkable declines in the cost of renewables that have made it quicker and cheaper to deploy renewable energy than to construct new nuclear power stations or fossil fuel plants (Lazard 2021: 3, IEA 2022, REN21 2022: 154), Japanese policymakers attempted to double down on nuclear power and to accelerate imports of hydrogen and ammonia from allies such as Australia. Once again, there was a telling (and belated) exception: after lagging behind in onshore wind power, where European firms had established a big lead, industrial policymakers, with a push from the LDP leadership, began to promote off-shore wind, where Japanese companies could exploit their formidable experience in building ships and maritime structures.

Part of the answer lies in genuine geographic and social barriers to the diffusion of renewable energy in Japan, and the continuing problem of intermittency – the sun does not always shine and the wind does not always blow – yet intermittency has not prevented renewables from achieving far higher levels of penetration elsewhere. Increasingly important were security concerns, which redoubled after the Senkaku boat collision incident in 2010 and especially after creation of the economic section in the National Security Council in 2020. The preference for nuclear power and hydrogen, and the reluctance to fully embrace renewables, reflected a particular conception of security in which energy should not only be produced domestically but, if at all possible, it should be based on centralized, dense, high-tech solutions under the control of big Japanese companies and amenable to export promotion.

This section will focus mainly on the relationship between industrial policy and electricity generation and will only briefly touch on other sectors or energy conservation technologies: electricity generation is by far the largest user of energy in Japan, accounting for 56 percent of all energy consumption in 2019 (METI 2022b: 78) and is poised to expand even further as electrification replaces fossil fuels in the effort to reduce emissions of carbon dioxide.

Energy Goals and Barriers

Japanese energy policy privileges four goals or criteria: *safety, energy security, economic efficiency,* and *environment,* or "S+3Es" (METI 2021a: 18–20). Safety takes into consideration the health consequences of pollution and accidents, including vulnerability to natural disasters. Economic security encompasses at least four dimensions: diversification by energy type and source; stability, including across time of day and year; ease of stockpiling; and domestic control, or at least control by diplomatic allies. Economic efficiency focuses on cost, though there are many ways to measure cost and always questions about how to incorporate environmental and other externalities. Environmental sustainability includes ambient pollution, such as sulfur dioxide, waste (ash, nuclear waste), and emissions of carbon dioxide and other greenhouse gases. Not explicitly included but ubiquitous in actual implementation is a "second S": ease of *siting,* including the amount of land required, the difficulty of acquiring it, and the distance from high-voltage transmission lines.

Applying these criteria to Japan immediately makes clear the daunting obstacles facing energy policy, especially expansion of renewable energy. Japan not only lacks fossil fuels but it is also only average in solar irradiance and onshore wind power potential (World Bank 2020: 36, IRENA 2022a: 4), which is compounded by Japan's difficult topography, including long, thin shape and mountainous terrain, and its high population density. Japan is also unusually susceptible to natural disasters, including earthquakes, typhoons, tsunami, and fires. The difficult terrain is compounded by isolation: as an island archipelago, Japan lacks adjacent electricity grids and for historical reasons the country is divided into two different electric frequencies: 60 Hz in the southwest and 50 Hz in the northeast.

Energy Sources and Carriers: What Are the Candidates?

Each of the potential energy sources has strengths and drawbacks. Japan relies most heavily on fossil fuels such as coal, oil, and liquified natural gas (LNG) and for good reason: they are widely available at reasonable, though sometimes volatile, prices; their generating plants take up little space; and the fuels themselves are easy to store and stockpile. Of course, their drawbacks are equally obvious: fossil fuels are almost entirely imported and emit huge amounts of greenhouse gases as well as conventional pollutants, which recent research shows to be much more damaging to human health than previously realized (WHO 2021).

Nuclear power, until Fukushima the second largest source of electricity, satisfies many of the criteria of concern to policymakers: it is dense (one compact power plant can generate stupendous amounts of electricity) and relatively clean, stable, and inexpensive. Unlike the case in France and the United States, from the 1970s to the Fukushima meltdown, construction of nuclear power plants in Japan did not exhibit cost inflation (Matsuo and Nei 2019). Nuclear fuel is compact and easy to store, and nuclear power seemed to be a promising technology export. Not surprisingly, Japan's 6th Strategic Energy Plan hails its virtues:

> Nuclear power is a low-carbon, semi-domestic energy source that can be sustained for several years using only domestically-owned fuels, and has excellent supply stability and efficiency. During operations it emits no greenhouse gases. Presuming that safety is assured, it is an important baseload power source that contributes to the long-term stability of the energy supply-demand structure. (METI 2021a: 35–36)

But particularly after Fukushima, two weaknesses of nuclear power were equally obvious. First, long construction times exacerbated high initial capital costs. And second, the public was concerned about safety. Statistically, nuclear power is extremely safe, but nuclear accidents are low probability/high risk events that are hard to evaluate ahead of time, as became stunningly evident in 2011. METI is well aware of these challenges:

> On the other hand, public trust in nuclear power generation has still not been fully earned due to a sense of insecurity, and a series of incidents, such as the

nuclear material protection incidents at TEPCO's Kashiwazaki-Kariwa Nuclear Power Station, have contributed to a lack of public confidence in nuclear power generation. In addition, various issues such as measures for spent fuel, nuclear fuel cycle, final disposal, and decommissioning of nuclear power plants, need to be addressed. (METI 2021a: 36)

The strengths and weaknesses of renewable energy reverse-mirror those of nuclear power. Construction times are short and capital costs are moderate, but stability is a problem: despite recent advances in battery and other forms of energy storage, renewable energy is still intermittent and expensive to store or stockpile. Wind and solar farms are low in density, which is a problem in crowded, mountainous Japan. Typhoons and lightning pose threats to renewables, as does the mismatch between the regions with the greatest energy potential (Hokkaido, Tohoku, and Kyushu) and the urban areas with the biggest demand and strongest grids (Tokyo, Nagoya, and Osaka).

A puzzling form of renewable energy is geothermal power, which has received relatively little attention from policymakers despite some highly attractive attributes. Geothermal is safe, purely domestic, generates electricity twenty-four hours a day, seven days a week, emits little carbon dioxide, and is relatively cheap. The main problem seems to be siting: most geothermal resources are located in or near national parks or *onsen* hot springs resorts, whose owners often complain of noise or reduced water pressure (Hymans 2021).

Winners through Fukushima

Until the triple disaster of Fukushima in 2011, most of the winners in Japanese electricity generation were related to industrial policy choices. About two-third of electricity generation came from burning of fossil fuels, first domestic coal and then imported coal and oil. Imported oil was cheap, particularly before the oil crises of the 1970s, flexible, and easy to stockpile. The government repeatedly tried to bring more energy imports under the control of Japanese companies, but without much success. After 1967, however, Japan did lead the world in creating and steadily expanding a market for liquefied natural gas (LNG).

With generous support from the government, Japan also steadily expanded its nuclear power system. By 2011, 54 reactors accounted for about 25 percent of national electricity generation, with an ultimate goal of reaching 50 percent or more.

For a time, government policy did favor one form of renewable energy: photovoltaic panels. After the oil shocks of the 1970s, the government poured money into research and subsidies for the deployment of solar panels, which were closely related to the flat panel displays in which Japanese companies were forging a global lead. Initially, however, high costs limited the share of solar energy.

After the oil shocks, the government also supported energy conservation, both in industry and in consumer products (Holroyd 2018). Japan's "top runner" program gained international attention for setting energy conservation targets on the basis of the most efficient Japanese products. Japan set high standards for vehicle efficiency and promoted the development of battery electric vehicles, hybrids, and then hydrogen fuel cell vehicles.

Three Potential Disruptors

Three developments threatened the equilibrium favoring fossil fuels and nuclear power: a political decision, a technology trend, and a disaster.

The political decision involved the choice to follow the global trend to deregulate the electricity supply industry. In the chaotic early days of electricity, private companies rushed to connect houses, stores, and factories with competing and reduplicative electricity lines. In the face of this wasteful and unstable chaos, governments in virtually all countries licensed utilities to generate, transmit, and distribute electricity within a fixed geographic area at a regulated price. For decades, these regulated monopolies provided stability, invested heavily, and assured universal access to electric power. The inflation of the 1970s, however, spurred economists and governments to seek alternative arrangements that could increase efficiency and cut costs. They concluded that electricity generation and, even at times, transmission were not actually natural monopolies. They began to allow entry of new generators and to require electric utilities to make their distribution networks available to competitors at equitable prices (OECD 2001).

Japan was a late and reluctant convert to the movement to deregulate electricity supply. Japan's system of ten regional electric utility monopolies combining generation, high-voltage transmission, and local distribution of electricity was the compromise outcome of a bitter and protracted political struggle in which the private utilities successfully fought off attempts to impose state ownership and control (Samuels 1987, Kikkawa 2004).

METI was reluctant and divided. Deregulation held the promise of cutting costs for Japanese firms at a time when their competitors abroad were gaining access to cheaper energy. It also promised, however, to result in far more players and far more complex markets. Nowhere in the world was the transition to competitive electricity markets entirely smooth, and at times it was highly disruptive, as exemplified by the infamous energy crisis that enveloped California in the summer of 2000 and led to the bankruptcies of Enron and the giant accounting firm Arthur Andersen (Tomain 2002). Moreover, the enhanced price pressures from competitive generation markets threatened to undermine the position of existing utilities and their nuclear power plants, and to favor dirty coal over cleaner alternatives.

Three rounds of revisions to the electricity business act between 1995 and 2003 enabled new generators to supply large, high-voltage customers such as factories, but the existing regional monopolies fiercely resisted expanding liberalization to include retail customers. To fend off further reform, they reduced electricity rates by sharply cutting investments in generation and transmission.

The Fukushima disaster and closing of nuclear power plants spurred further reforms. In January 2012, METI convened an Expert Committee on Electricity Systems Reform. With the return to power of the LDP, the Diet passed legislation in 2013 to liberalize the retail sector by 2016. Analysts noted that "transmission and distribution will not be separated, but regarded as one function, referred to as 'network' companies in the language of the Japanese reform. The approach is unique in Japan and very different from what is in place in Europe or the US, where transmission and distribution are separate" (Goto and Sueyoshi 2016: 18). The result was three categories of licenses: generation, transmission-distribution, and retail. The legislation called for the establishment of a wholesale power market, separate accounting for the network sector, and the creation of a neutral organization to monitor network operations. In 2015, further legislation created the Electricity and Gas Market Surveillance Commission and an alliance of the ten traditional regional electricity utilities (plus J-Power and the Japan Electric Power Company) called the Organization for Cross-regional Coordination of Transmission Operators, Japan. Both organizations were put under the supervision of METI despite the trend, both globally and in Japan, of creating independent regulatory commissions.

Under the new arrangements, utilities still controlled final distribution of electricity to homes and shops and enjoyed virtually free rein to charge high connection rates and to limit new connections from rival generators, especially those using solar or wind power, on the grounds that they might unsettle the balance of regional supply and demand. New entrants, including telecom companies and local governments, did appear, mostly just reselling energy from existing companies with more flexible and attractive rate plans, but few made big inroads: the share of nonutility generation stagnated at just over 10 percent (JEPIC 2022: 61) and the steep increase in fuel prices attending Russia's invasion of Ukraine in 2022 pushed many of the new providers out of the market (*Nikkei Asia*, December 10, 2022).

More important were cross-entry and new business tie-ups by existing utilities. Electric and gas utilities began competing with each other and offering customers gas and electric power as a package. Tokyo Electric Power and Chubu Electric Power, two of the largest utilities, formed a joint venture called JERA to merge their thermal power generating operations. Thus, despite several rounds of dramatic market liberalization, the basic structure of giant domestic energy utilities monitored and regulated by METI remained intact.

A second major factor potentially challenging the dominance of fossil fuels and nuclear power was a reduction in the cost of renewables (Lazard 2021: 3), though the decline was less dramatic in Japan than elsewhere, especially for wind power (IRENA 2022d: 64, 75, 88–89, 119). The Japanese government had a long history of supporting photovoltaics and from the early 1990s provided hefty subsidies for residential installation of solar panels. By the early 2000s, Japanese companies captured about half of the global market for solar panels, and in 2006 and 2007, Japan boasted the second largest installation of solar photovoltaic capacity in the world, trailing only Germany (IRENA 2015: 24–26).

After Fukushima, the DPJ government introduced a Feed-in-Tariff (FIT) scheme in 2012 that allowed owners of solar panels to sell excess electricity back to the electric utilities at a very generous rate. The measure succeeded in further stimulating deployment of solar panels but locked in high expenses that put upward pressure on household electricity bills. Just about that time, the Chinese government lavished huge subsidies on the manufacture of solar panels, attracting a swarm of new entrants. Fierce domestic competition pushed Chinese firms to cut costs and export excess capacity, driving the cost of solar energy below that of conventional energy sources and devastating Japanese and German manufacturers of solar panels. In 2011, the average sales price of solar panels in Japan was ¥180 per watt; a decade later, the average price declined to ¥48 (REI 2023).

With the cost of FIT subsidies rising rapidly and the benefits increasingly flowing to Chinese suppliers, METI steadily reduced the FIT rate for new projects and introduced an auction system for all new large projects. In some ways, the auctions succeeded, attracting many bidders and resulting in steadily declining prices. But few projects were completed, the rate of cost cutting declined, and prices remained much higher than in other countries. The culprits included the high cost of land acquisition and difficulties securing grid connections, but a major barrier was the high cost of Japanese hardware: as of 2019, half of modules and three-quarters of DC-AC inverters installed were procured domestically even as the Japanese share of global production melted away (IRENA 2021: 17–22).

If cost cutting in solar energy was less dramatic than in other leading countries, the pace of expansion of onshore wind power was positively glacial (Bossler 2012, Mizuno 2014). Despite some highly attractive attributes – clean, safe, secure, potentially very low in cost, and complementary with solar power (since wind tends to blow more at night) – wind power was not included in the initial sunshine program of 1974. Wind did receive R&D support after 1978 but the amounts were lower and less stable than those allocated to other renewables. Capital subsidies starting in 1998 supported a small boom in wind power, but leveled off after the early 2000s. METI energy plans began to take wind somewhat more seriously from 2008 as declines in cost powered wind installations abroad, but siting remained difficult, regulation strict, and scale very limited. METI did not approach relaxation of safety regulations as zealously as it did with hydrogen fueling stations. Windmills were considered as "buildings" under Japan's strict construction codes, a full-time electrician was required to be on site, and wind farms were excluded from agricultural land (IRENA 2021: 23). Ironically, Japanese wind companies earned two-third of their revenues abroad and in 2008 industry leader Mitsubishi Heavy Industries suspended sales of wind turbines in Japan. As an industry, the Japanese wind sector was becalmed.

Attention then shifted offshore. Japan had significant potential offshore wind resources, but the geography was difficult, with deep offshore waters. As with onshore wind, Japanese companies started to develop more promising overseas locations. Notably, from 2013 to 2020 Mitsubishi formed a joint venture in Denmark with global wind leader Vestas. The joint venture actively explored projects in Europe and Taiwan. Around 2020, as new technology developments made offshore wind more economically viable, METI re-examined the possibility of exporting wind technology to Asia, especially for floating wind turbines (Public-Private Council on Enhancement of Industrial Competitiveness for Offshore Wind Power Generation 2020).

In sum, as of the early 2020s, the Japanese wind power industry, both onshore and offshore, failed to take wing. This disappointing outcome resulted from the interaction of geographic and social problems with siting and, until around 2019, the perception that wind power was ill-suited to Japan and had little chance of developing into an export industry. The favored child was still nuclear power.

Cost cutting was less evident in the geothermal sector and output barely increased. Given the many advantages of geothermal power – safety, stability, low cost, domestic ownership, lack of pollution, and greenhouse gasses – it is puzzling that Japan has not pushed harder to craft more productive compromises to promote it. Japan is third in the world in geothermal resources, but ranks only ninth in actual production (METI 2022b: 100). It appears that geothermal energy, a decentralized, low-tech form of renewable energy, with few prospects for exports, is less attractive to industrial policymakers.

The third disruptive factor, of course, was the Fukushima nuclear accident in 2011 and subsequent shutdown of all of Japan's nuclear reactors, most of which remained off-line a decade later. Not surprisingly, after Fukushima, public opinion shifted against nuclear power and citizens groups filed many lawsuits to prevent nuclear restarts. After negotiations between the outgoing DPJ government and the incoming LDP regime, responsibility for nuclear safety regulation was taken from METI and entrusted to a new, semi-independent Nuclear Regulation Authority under the Ministry of the Environment with a largely new staff not connected with the previous regulatory regime. The new Authority proved surprisingly tough, imposing stricter safety standards that resulted in sharply higher costs and effectively rendered it uneconomical to restart many of the nuclear reactors (Koppenborg 2023). To make up for the lost capacity, electric utilities were forced to burn more coal and liquefied natural gas.

Even after the three disruptions of the 2010s, Japan remained more reliant than ever on fossil fuels, and far more dependent than its European counterparts, as documented in the table below. Coal and LNG accounted for 70 percent of total electricity supply in 2020. Solar power expanded significantly, but still accounted for less than 8 percent of total electricity generation. Wind and geothermal energy remained insignificant, as did nuclear power.

Electricity sources: fossil fuels, nuclear power and renewables before and after Fukushima

	Japan 2010	Japan 2020	France 2021–22	Germany 2021–22
Coal	27.8%	31.0%	1%	33%
Oil, etc.	8.6%	6.4%	0%	0%
Natural gas [Japan: all LNG]	29.0%	39.0%	10%	11%
Sub-total: fossil fuels	*65.4%*	*76.4%*	*11%*	*44%*
Nuclear	25.1%	3.9%	68%	9%
Hydro	7.3%	7.8%	10%	4%
Solar	0.3%	7.9%	2%	5%
Wind	0.3%	0.9%	8%	30%
Geothermal	0.2%	0.3%	NA	NA
Biomass (incl. trash)	1.3%	2.9%	0%	7%
Sub-total: Renewables (except hydro)	*2.1%*	*12.0%*	*10%*	*42%*

Sources: (METI ANRE 2022: 28); (REI 2022b: 図 6).

Back to the Future: Renewed Promotion of Nuclear Power

In the end, the three potential disruptors failed to fundamentally shift the course of Japanese energy policy. In the first national election after returning to power, the LDP downplayed its commitment to nuclear power. Once he was returned to power, however, Prime Minister Abe claimed a mandate to promote a range of policies he had not run on during the campaign, including restarts of nuclear power plants (Pekkanen, Reed, and Scheiner 2016).

Lawsuits by civil society groups and rigorous screening by the Nuclear Regulation Authority slowed the actual pace of restarts but two new developments restored a sense of urgency. First, international pressure to join the movement to reduce emissions of greenhouse gases grew more intense. In late 2020, Abe's successor Suga Yoshihide used his maiden speech to the Diet to commit Japan to reducing net greenhouse gas emissions to zero by 2050. He mentioned the importance of innovations such as next-generation solar cells and carbon recycling, but the main thrust was that Japan would re-invigorate nuclear power. Second, Russia's invasion of Ukraine in February 2022 reignited concerns about relying on volatile and expensive imported energy.

In response, Suga's successor, Fumio Kishida, unveiled a "green transformation" (GX) plan drafted by METI to enhance energy security and industrial competitiveness. After being somewhat sidelined under Suga, current and former METI officials assumed important positions under Kishida's cabinet and pressed the cause of nuclear power (*Nikkei Asia*, October 8, 2021). METI also succeeded in re-establishing influence over the Nuclear Regulation Authority: by July 2022, "former METI officials occupied the top three senior official positions in the NRA's secretariat" (Kamikawa 2024). Enhancing national security was a major goal of the new "green transformation" plan: officials feared that without revitalization of nuclear power, "Japan would run the risk of losing human resources and technological capabilities, falling behind in important areas like energy security and national competitiveness. This was particularly concerning as Russia and China looked to take the lead in the building of next-generation reactors" (Kamikawa 2024). The plan touched on renewables and demand response, but focused on expanding nuclear power, including construction of new reactors, a complete reversal of immediate post-Fukushima policy (*Nikkei* August 24, 2022, December 23, 2022) (Ohta and Barrett 2023).

METI's nuclear plans involved three elements. *First, develop and commercialize next-generation nuclear reactors,* including

(1) innovative light-water reactors with enhanced safety features,
(2) small modular reactors (SMRs) with a standardized design suitable for being sited almost anywhere, and

(3) high-temperature gas reactors (HTGR) capable of producing hydrogen as well as electric power (*Nikkei* November 23, 2022).

Second, accelerate restarts of existing nuclear facilities that had already been cleared by the NRA but were stalled by local opposition by "strengthening support" for surrounding local communities (presumably by increasing already-lavish subsidies) and intensifying "public relations" and "communication" with the wider public (Nuclear Sub-Committee 2022: 3–4). *Third, extend operating licenses of existing facilities.* The draft report of the Cabinet Secretariat's GX [Green Transformation] Implementation Committee called for extending licenses: "Similar to the current system, the [initial] operating period would be 40 years, with a 20-year limit on the period during which extensions are allowed, and additional extensions would be limited to the time reactors were out of operation" after Fukushima while awaiting permission to restart (Cabinet Secretariat GX Implementation Committee 2022: 7).

One favorable change was the degree of public acceptance. In the immediate aftermath of Fukushima, popular resistance to nuclear restarts remained firm, but after 2020, perhaps because of the economic dislocation surrounding the COVID pandemic, opposition began to soften. After Russia's invasion of Ukraine in February 2022 and the government's announcement of new nuclear plans in August 2022, about half the public came to support proposals to rebuild or expand nuclear plants, though reported responses varied significantly by pollster and wording of the questions (*Asahi*, February 22, 2022; *Yomiuri*, September 4, 2022; *NHK* December 13, 2022).

Still, these ambitious nuclear plans faced a number of challenges that left many observers skeptical that Japan could restore nuclear power's share of electricity generation to the 20–22 percent foreseen in the Sixth Basic Energy Plan of 2021 (METI 2021a: 106); (*Nikkei* December 23, 2022). As the reports acknowledged, Japan still lacked facilities to recycle or dispose of nuclear waste. Many local communities still vehemently opposed nuclear power. Long lead times for nuclear permitting and construction cut against the need to take immediate action against global warming. Technological uncertainty cast a long shadow: small modular reactors have been the technology of the future for decades but they were still not approved for construction, cost estimates varied widely and showed ominous signs of inflation, and the prospects for reaching international agreements to winnow out the plethora of technologies and designs to attain "series economies" in manufacturing and deployment did not seem bright (Murakami and Anbumozhi 2021: 63–67) (*New York Times*, November 12, 2023).

One potential compromise would be to put new reactors on existing sites, possibly replacing decommissioned reactors, but this implied a potentially serious tension between building new reactors and restarting existing plants or extending their licenses. Excepting cases where the Nuclear Regulation Authority demanded significant investments in safety, the marginal operating cost of restarting or extending the life of existing facilities would be far lower than that of new nuclear plants, or indeed virtually any other energy source. Unless the government provided huge and unpopular subsidies, utilities would be tempted to say "thank you for the restarts and extensions" and refrain from investing in the fancy but expensive and unproven new technologies promoted by METI, the LDP, and the nuclear experts. Professor Kikkawa Takeo, a leading expert on the economics of the Japanese electricity industry, was blunt: "The business community wants to extend operations. It seems as if METI has come up with the idea of building new nuclear power plants as a distraction. If a plant is to be replaced, there is no need to extend its operation, and it is likely that METI has come up with the idea in a half-baked manner" (*Asahi* September 18, 2022).

Extending Fossil Fuels: The Push to Use Hydrogen and Ammonia in Electricity Generation

Political leaders, energy policymakers, and the influential automobile industry have come to embrace hydrogen as another high-tech solution to Japan's S+3Es energy dilemmas. Hydrogen is a *medium* to transmit and store energy rather than a primary energy *source*. In that sense it is more similar to a battery than to coal or oil, though it is far easier to transport or to store for long periods. Hydrogen can be used to power fuel cells that combine hydrogen with oxygen from the air to produce energy and water, emitting neither conventional pollutants nor greenhouse gases, or it can be burned, either by itself or in combination with other fuels, to generate electricity.

The problem is that hydrogen rarely occurs in its elemental form, so it must be extracted from a hydrogen compound, usually water (H_2O) or a fossil fuel such as methane (CH_4), the principal component of natural gas. Electrolysis of water by renewable energy such as wind or solar power would be ideal, as proponents of hydrogen tend to highlight, but remains prohibitively expensive. In practice, hydrogen is usually produced either as a byproduct of various industrial processes, in which case it is moderate in price but limited in quantity, or through high-temperature "steam reforming" of natural gas. Reforming is still expensive, and produces both pollutants and greenhouse gases.

Lacking sufficient hydrogen domestically, Japanese firms explored various compounds containing hydrogen that could be transported by sea as a liquid, including liquid hydrogen, organic hydrides, and ammonia. Electric utilities were initially skeptical of hydrogen, but saw more promise in ammonia (NH_3) for its ability to "carry" hydrogen more compactly and inexpensively than compressed or cryogenic hydrogen, largely using existing infrastructure. As Professor Kikkawa noted, "The electricity industry is particularly keen on ammonia. They have a lot of coal-fired plants that are highly cost-competitive but emit a lot of greenhouse gases. If they can burn ammonia together with coal then they can reduce the criticism of those plants and keep them operating as long as possible" (*Financial Times*, July 22, 2022).

Little more than a month after Suga's commitment that Japan would attain carbon neutrality by 2050, METI unveiled a "green growth" strategy aiming to make environmental policy into growth policy (METI 2021b). The third supplemental budget of 2020 had allocated 2 trillion yen (about $17 billion) to the creation of a Green Innovation Fund under METI-NEDO, supplemented by tax breaks, government-mediated financing, and help with standardization, deregulation, and international contacts. The new strategy laid out fourteen priority areas for financial support. The first five sectors all involved energy, two of them for hydrogen and ammonia:

1) Offshore wind
2) Fuel ammonia
3) Hydrogen
4) Nuclear power
5) Automobile and battery

The next month, NEDO announced a ¥60 billion (about $520 million) plan to support creation of a "green" ammonia supply chain (Atchison 2022, NEDO 2022). Major projects included a 50 percent–50 percent ammonia-coal co-firing demonstration at Hekinan power plant; three joint industry-academic teams competing against each other to develop improved ammonia synthesis catalysts; and efforts to commercialize a 100 percent ammonia-fed, two MW gas turbine.

Despite its appeal as a way of extending the life of existing coal-burning plants, ammonia faced several challenges, including ensuring safety, securing supplies, cutting prices, and reducing pollution. Although ammonia does not emit CO_2 when burned, the fossil fuels used to produce it do, along with NOx. A detailed analysis by Bloomberg New Energy Finance concluded:

> The levelized cost of electricity (LCOE) for a typical Japanese coal plant retrofitted for ammonia co-firing at 50% or higher energy content is significantly higher than zero-emission sources such as offshore wind . . . Even with

green ammonia, at co-firing rates of 50% or lower, CO_2 emissions from
a retrofitted coal plant would still be worse than a natural gas fueled combined
cycle gas turbine. (BloombergNEF 2022: 7, 11)

BloombergNEF concluded that the limited supplies of ammonia could be better
used to produce fertilizer, power shipping, or supply seasonal balancing for
electricity generation.

Conclusion

Why would a country deeply uneasy about reliance on imported energy slack
off on developing renewable energy, and why would a government facing
widespread opposition to nuclear power after the Fukushima nuclear disaster
insist on redoubling its commitments to reopening shuttered nuclear power
plants and building new ones?

Part of the answer clearly involves drawbacks to renewables, particularly in
Japan, and particularly before the steep decline in the cost of renewables in the
late 2010s. Intermittency is still a significant problem and siting renewables is
particularly difficult in Japan, given its isolation, mountainous terrain, frag-
mented electrical grid, and susceptibility to natural disasters. Nuclear power, in
contrast, is relatively compact, stable, and inexpensive. In particular, restarting
or extending the operating life of existing nuclear plants is economically
appealing (as long as any required safety upgrades are not too onerous), since
the capital cost has already been incurred. Next-generation reactors hold the
hope of lower costs, though the nuclear power industry's history of chronic
delays and cost overruns strongly suggests the case for caution.

For all the impact of the three disruptors (reluctant electricity deregulation,
steep declines in the cost of renewable energy, and the Fukushima nuclear
disaster) and all the government's bold talk of promoting a green transformation
("GX"), policy remains remarkably committed to the continuation of nuclear
power and fossil fuels. The first five sectors mentioned in METI's green growth
strategy all involved energy, but only offshore wind could be considered
"green," and it received far less attention than the revival of nuclear power
and the development of hydrogen and ammonia as energy carriers.

If generic problems with renewable power and Japan's particular geographic
situation explain some of the preference for nuclear power (and recently
hydrogen/ammonia) over renewables, industrial policy and increasing concerns
about national security clearly play major roles as well. The preference for
nuclear power and hydrogen reflects a conception of security as best assured
by complex, centralized, high tech, long-term solutions under the control of
Japanese companies. The exception that proves the rule is solar energy, a form

of renewable energy that *was* favored by industrial policy in the early years, when a handful of Japanese electronics companies dominated the industry. But when subsidized Chinese solar panels flooded into Japan, policymakers cooled on solar power. Wind power could become a new exception, if the lukewarm attitude toward onshore wind gives way to sustained support for offshore wind and the possibility of exports of Japanese technology.

5 Technology for Economic National Security: Promotion, Bailouts, and Onshoring

As the preceding sections have shown, much of the industrial policy machinery – personnel, budgets, systems of consultation with business, political stability (with only two brief breaks) – is still in place. To be sure, the demand for and supply of preferential financing is reduced from the past, and relations with the business community are not quite as tight as they had been up through the 1990s, but the demand for policy support has actually increased, particularly after the sudden rise of concern for "economic security" in the early 2020s, and the ability to supply it remains formidable, as seen in the big supplemental budgets of 2020–23.

The problem is that the private sector is weaker than it was in the rapid growth period of the 1960s and 1970s or during the financial bubble of the 1980s, making the task of supporting it far more difficult. Rather than picking winners, the government often finds itself trying to prop up former winners or to smooth their transition to a new future. The heady days in which Japanese corporations dismissed government as a pesky interference (Callon 1995) have long passed. Japanese companies retain formidable strengths in some sectors, such as fine chemicals for semiconductors and specialized parts for cell phones, and more start-up companies are emerging, but they are not sufficient to propel the economy, as the slow pace of economic growth and still-modest rates of new business formation testify (Katz 2023).

METI has striven to uphold Japan's advantage in high-skill production, both to maintain growth and employment and to enhance economic security. We can observe major initiatives in areas of traditional METI responsibility and Japanese competitiveness, such as automobiles and batteries, steel, aerospace, and electronics, but few unambiguous successes and little movement in other areas identified as having great potential, including bio-technology and software, partly because they do not fit unambiguously under METI's ambit and have not actually received much policy support. In the face of increased competition from Japan's nimbler and lower-cost neighbors, we can also observe a temptation (on the part of both industry and METI) to reach for long-term technical solutions, often protected by a thicket of intellectual property rights, and a narrow vision of Japan's competitive advantage as residing in systems integration rather than in speed, cost-cutting, or innovation. In this section, we review developments and obstacles in areas identified as priorities in METI visions and budgets.

Aerospace and the Appeal of Systems Integration

Japan's protracted effort to promote the aerospace industry is an example not so much of picking a winner or sustaining a winner but of trying to reignite a former winner, with at best mixed and ambiguous results. During World War II, the Japanese aerospace industry designed and produced some impressive aircraft, notably the famed Mitsubishi "Zero" fighter plane. Japan fell behind world trends in aircraft design under the American Occupation, which banned work on aerospace, but soon after Japan regained its independence in 1952, MITI promoted a plan to build a sixty-passenger turbo-prop (Mercado 1995). The YS-11 project (1954–74) created an unwieldy national company in which the government held a majority share and the resulting plane was slow to market. After steep financial losses and the appreciation of the yen in the wake of the dissolution of the Bretton Woods international monetary system, the project was finally discontinued.

Successor projects continue to bubble up, however, including an effort to replace the aging Mitsubishi F1 fighter plane with an-all Japanese replacement dubbed the FSX (later named the F2). The United States objected that the project would be a wasteful impediment to defense cooperation and pressed the Japanese government to co-develop a variation of the American F-16. The Japanese side objected to the American black-boxing of key technology, but under pressure from the American Congress, it finally acquiesced to a joint-development deal in 1989 (Noble 1992). Even as efforts at independent development of new planes faltered, from the 1980s Japanese aerospace companies experienced rapid growth as major subcontractors to Boeing and Airbus (Friedman and Samuels 1993).

The bursting of the financial bubble and the economic turbulence of the 1990s then stimulated a period of reflection. METI's Industrial Structure Council, building on the work of Stanford economist Aoki Masahiko on comparative capitalism and the University of Tokyo business specialist Fujimoto Takahiro on product architectures, attempted to sketch out the areas in which Japanese companies had the greatest competitive potential. Fujimoto, who had carried out extensive research at Toyota, convinced many academics and practitioners that products varied along two key dimensions: closed versus open and integrated versus modular (Fujimoto 2004). The United States, with its fluid labor and capital markets, had an advantage at open and modular products such as personal computers, with their plug-and-play interfaces, while Japan, with its permanent employment system and tightly aligned subcontracting systems, excelled at the close interaction required to make high-quality, closed, and integral products, such as cars.

METI and industry agreed that airplanes, which integrate hundreds of thousands of parts, presented a promising application (Ozaki 2012). The market for regional jets with thirty to fifty seats (later increased to seventy to ninety seats at the insistence of potential clients JAL and ANA) was particularly enticing because of the expansion of Tokyo's Haneda airport and the lack of competing models from Boeing and Airbus. Defense applications were a secondary, but ever-present, consideration. In 2003 METI invited proposals for an R&D project. Mitsubishi Heavy Industries, the only applicant, then formed a consortium with Fuji Heavy Industries, Japan Aircraft Development Corporation (JADC), and Japan Aerospace Exploratory Agency (JAXA). Repeated delays left Mitsubishi behind Brazilian rival Embraer, which proved more adept at using international aerospace engineers. Mitsubishi's SpaceJet never managed to acquire type certification from regulators and the project was suspended in late 2020 amid the sharp downturn in air travel due to the COVID-19 pandemic (*Nikkei*, October 23, 2020). In early 2023, Mitsubishi announced that it would liquidate its passenger jet subsidiary.

Despite this setback, the appeal of aerospace remained undiminished. Japan was soon in negotiations, first with the United States and then with Britain, to have a Mitsubishi-led consortium co-develop a successor to the F2 fighter plane (*Nikkei*, May 17, 2022).

Automobiles: The Long and Uncertain Transition to New Powerplants

The automobile industry, with its "closed and integral" product architecture, is Japan's largest and most successful industrial sector, but like automakers everywhere, Japanese car companies are struggling to navigate the long transition away from internal combustion engines. Industrial policy has played a significant role in supporting that transition.

Observers often contend that the Japanese automobile industry grew up without government support and indeed in the face of government interference, notably a failed attempt to consolidate the industry in the late 1950s (Henderson 1983: 113). This contention is deeply flawed. Consolidation was not a complete failure, considerable financial support was extended first to assemblers and then to parts makers, and up through the early 1980s, the industry enjoyed virtually complete protection against imports and foreign investment (Mutoh

1988, Yamazaki 2003). Of course, protection is no guarantee of success, and Japanese automakers did indeed come to excel at the design and production of cars, particularly engines and transmissions, the most complex and intricate automotive mechanisms (Misawa 2005).

No sooner had they achieved global mastery, however, than the Japanese auto industry confronted pressure to improve and then replace conventional internal combustion engines. From the late 1960s, the international environmental movement lobbied for increasingly stringent restrictions on emissions, first of conventional pollutants and then of carbon dioxide, while the oil shocks of the 1970s revealed Japan's vulnerability to fluctuations in the availability and price of imported energy. Even before the first oil crisis, METI began to promote development of battery-powered electric vehicles (BEVs), including support for research and development, standardization, charging infrastructure, and market expansion through subsidies for leasing and purchases. Limitations in the battery technology of the 1970s–1980s prevented BEVs from making inroads into the automotive market, but in the 1990s, when California suddenly introduced draconian pollution control requirements, Toyota was able to use the experience it had accumulated to introduce leading-edge hybrid electric vehicles using small batteries (Åhman 2006).

METI renewed efforts to promote full battery-powered electric vehicles in 2009–10, when Mitsubishi and Nissan introduced the first mass-market BEVs (notably the Nissan LEAF). METI provided big subsidies for production and purchase of batteries and for building charging infrastructure, and promoted the "all-Japanese" CHAdeMO charging format, introduced in 2010 by Tokyo Electric Power and five Japanese automakers, as an international standard. METI's ability to coordinate and support multiple technologies was especially impressive given deep divisions within the industry between the BEV camp, led by Nissan and Mitsubishi, and the hybrid/fuel cell camp headed by Toyota and including Honda. Electric vehicles, however, were still constrained. They suffered from high costs, short range, and slow charging rates, as well as a still-inadequate charging infrastructure. Consumer demand for battery-powered electric vehicles proved anemic.

METI had promoted research on hydrogen fuel cells as early as the Sunshine Project and the Moonlight Project launched in the 1970s. The government accelerated support under Prime Ministers Obuchi and Koizumi, including the Japan Hydrogen and Fuel Cell Demonstration (JHFC) Project begun in 2002, helping Japan to establish a big lead in hydrogen-related patents (Ishitani and Baba 2008, Behling 2013). Like battery-powered vehicles, fuel cells emitted no pollution or carbon dioxide but they also possessed two major advantages over BEVs: longer range and much quicker refueling speeds. Yet serious obstacles remained: (1) Costs of fuel, stations, and on-board fuel cells remained high. (2) Hydrogen suffered from a severe chicken-and-egg problem: without an adequate network of stations there was little demand for hydrogen vehicles and without robust sales of vehicles there was no demand to construct fueling stations. (3) In practice, hydrogen vehicles were far from clean: the vast majority of available hydrogen came not from "green" renewable energy but from natural gas, either with or without carbon capture and storage ("blue" and "gray" hydrogen, respectively).

Once Toyota introduced a serious fuel cell vehicle in 2015, government shifted emphasis to the strategy favored by Toyota and Honda: hybrids today, hydrogen fuel cell vehicles tomorrow (Behling, Williams, and Managi 2016). METI, supported by LDP leaders led by Prime Minister Abe and in close cooperation with industry (especially Toyota), worked hard to remove impediments. The ministry allocated hundreds of millions of dollars for hydrogen-related research and heavily subsidized stations and fuel. METI strove to reduce the cost of constructing stations by relaxing safety requirements, often in the face of considerable popular resistance. Japan devised numerous plans to import low-cost hydrogen fuel, though at least at first, it was overwhelmingly gray.

Unfortunately for all the grandiose talk by Prime Minister Abe and others about creating a "hydrogen society" by about 2020, developments abroad made it increasingly clear that hydrogen was losing the clean vehicle race. Thanks to the entry of ambitious new entrants such as the American start-up Tesla and numerous Chinese makers of automotive batteries and "new energy vehicles," often with significant government support, the design and production of battery-powered electric vehicles displayed marked improvements in cost, range, charging speed, safety, and charging infrastructure. Numerous governments in Europe and North America announced that by 2030 or 2035 they would ban the sale of cars powered by internal combustion engines, casting a huge shadow over the Japanese strategy of relying on hybrid vehicles for the indefinite future. Toyota and Honda produced few pure battery-electric vehicles, while Nissan, the Japanese carmaker most committed to electric cars, was distracted by conflicts with partner Renault and the spectacular legal imbroglio surrounding former boss Carlos Ghosn.

Despite the cost-cutting efforts of Toyota and the Japanese government, hydrogen fuel, stations, and fuel cells remained expensive, and the infrastructure completely inadequate. In 2021, six years after the commencement of mass marketing, only about 14,000 hydrogen fuel cell vehicles were sold globally, just over half of them in South Korea, compared to millions of battery electric vehicles. Ninety-eight percent came from just two models – industry leader Hyundai's Nexo and Toyota's Mirai (Munoz 2022) – and those were heavily discounted. Japan hosted only about 160 hydrogen fuel stations, all highly subsidized and many operating only part time (REI 2022a: 35). To reach the goal of rough parity with gasoline prices by 2030, hydrogen costs would have to decline by two-thirds (Arias 2019: 14).

As of the early 2020s, only small volumes of green hydrogen were produced and immediate prospects for expanding production were limited. This led environmental groups to charge that amidst the dearth of hydrogen of all types, the government had been promoting the wrong form of hydrogen (gray or blue rather than green) for the wrong (i.e., low priority) applications, such as passenger vehicles and home heating (IRENA 2022b, REI 2022a: 21–22). By the time green hydrogen, and or any hydrogen at all, becomes available in large quantities, it may well be too late for hydrogen fuel cells to compete in any vehicle classes, with the possible exception of large trucks.

In the case of automobiles, METI did not seek to pick winners or reduce technological diversity. Rather, it tried, and continues to try, to contribute to the evolution of entire infrastructures conducive to the transition to cleaner, more energy efficient cars, whether they be powered by hybrids, batteries, or hydrogen fuel cells. However, when Nissan and Mitsubishi, the main proponents of battery electric vehicles, fell behind Toyota and Honda, leaders of the "hybrids today, hydrogen tomorrow" faction, government policy came to favor hydrogen cars, based on a fossil fuel infrastructure, over EVs, in which Chinese automakers surged to a lead in both manufacturing efficiency and innovation, particularly for batteries and software.

Japanese industrial policy scrambled to catch up. METI and the land ministry issued a 163-page draft policy setting a goal of capturing 30 percent of the global market for next-generation "software-defined [electric] vehicles" by 2030, largely by encouraging collective efforts by leading Japanese assemblers such as Toyota and Honda to train more software engineers and develop artificial intelligence and semiconductors for the auto industry. Despite paying lip service to entry from startup firms and allied industries, the emphasis was clearly on helping Japanese assemblers to catch up with new trends in the global auto industry (METI and MLITT 2024).

METI did not set out to pick a winning technology, but to back the domestic industry. Unfortunately, the industry grew narrower and lacked dynamic new entrants such as America's Tesla. The automotive case suggests that one of Japan's strengths, strong and persistent support of technological breakthroughs, such as hydrogen fuel cells, can limit flexibility in the absence of innovative new firms. The automotive case may also reveal the limits to industrial policies – and corporate strategies – that rely heavily on closed architectures, patents, and avoidance of price competition.

Green Steel: A Good but Tough Case for Promoting the Transition to Hydrogen

The steel industry is another case of industrial policy seeking to maintain the competitive position of a leading industry facing new challenges. Steel is central to the Japanese economy, business community, and METI, and a major contributor of campaign funds to the LDP. Like autos, steel is a sophisticated industry producing high-quality products. It consistently runs a big trade surplus and engages in extensive overseas investments. It has no trouble accessing markets or capital.

Steel's problem is environmental: steel production results in large amounts of pollutants and it accounts for about 14 percent of Japan's emissions of CO_2. The industry has a long history of working with government to reduce pollution, but when Prime Minister Suga suddenly pledged in October 2020 that Japan would join the international movement to reach "zero carbon" by 2050, steel found itself in a difficult position. No readily available technology exists to produce carbon-neutral steel. The high temperatures required to produce steel make it difficult to rely on electricity, and at any rate, Japanese industry pays high electricity prices.

Steel is thus a high-priority candidate for the use of hydrogen, which can burn at high temperatures (IRENA 2022b: 30). Adapting hydrogen to steel production will not be easy, however, and the industry released a desperate plea for help:

> Hydrogen-based iron making is an iron making process that is totally different from the existing blast furnace process which we have reached over several thousand years in history ... We request the government to adopt the following policies to support the realization of zero-carbon steel:
>
> –Strong and continuous national support by the Japanese government for medium- to long-term technological development of extremely difficult hurdle [*sic*], and establishment of a national strategy for decarbonization, including the development of social infrastructure for the stable supply of large quantities of carbon-free hydrogen and carbon-free electricity at low cost and social implementation of CCUS [Carbon Capture, Usage and Storage] in an economically rational manner ...
>
> –Financial support for the practical application and implementation of the results of technological development ...
>
> –Ensuring equal footing where Japan's industries are not disadvantaged in international competition. (JISF 2021)

METI's NEDO unit engaged in joint research and demonstration projects with industry leaders Nippon Steel and JFE Steel to substitute hydrogen for some or all of the coke used to chemically reduce iron to steel. But industry leaders complained that METI support through 2030 was scheduled to total less than $1.5 billion, a small fraction of the $72 billion they estimated would be required to make a full transition to hydrogen-based "green steel" (*Nikkei* July 16, 2022). In other words, far from opposing or denigrating industrial policy, they wanted more of it. And rather than lobbying for protection against imports, they sought to enhance their ability to compete internationally.

Double-Duty: Export Promotion as Diplomacy *and* Industrial Policy

For decades, Japanese policy has sought to promote exports, both as a way of supporting Japanese industry and as a way to advance Japan's diplomatic and foreign policy goals, notably in the form of foreign aid to Southeast Asia, where Japan competes with China for influence. A new version of this tendency appeared in several sectors in the early 2000s. METI and other parts of the government attempted to take advantage of the global enthusiasm for Japanese popular culture, and the new academic concept of "soft power," by creating a "Cool Japan" program to expand exports of media 'contents' industries such as manga, anime, and electronic games. Despite direct supervision by the cabinet after 2010 and the expenditure of hundreds of millions of dollars, positive results were hard to find, and observers agreed that the government was ill-suited to the promotion of culture-based creative industries (Kawashima 2018, Otmazgin 2020).

In Abe Shinzo's second term as prime minister, attention shifted to more traditional areas. In 2013 his cabinet vowed to triple exports of infrastructure. But once again, success proved elusive. Japanese costs were high, acquiring land was often difficult and controversial, and extended construction times left projects vulnerable to political reversals.

Some initiatives fell prey to environmental and safety concerns. In the case of coal, for example, the Japanese government pointed to the rapid increase in demand for energy in developing countries, and claimed that restricting exports of Japan's "supercritical" and "ultra supercritical" steam turbines for electricity generation could 'crowd-in' less efficient turbines procured domestically or imported from China. Environmental critics pointed out the Chinese boilers were not necessarily less efficient and emphasized that *any* construction of coal plants would lead to carbon lock-in (WWF 2015). In a 2021 meeting of the G7 leading industrial nations, the Japanese government agreed in principle to stop supporting exports of coal plants, but METI insisted on retaining a big loophole for coal plants that include arrangements intended to reduce emissions, such as carbon capture and storage (for which economically viable projects have yet to appear) or combined combustion with ammonia (METI 2021c). Nevertheless, both the government-owned Japan Bank for International Cooperation and private Japanese banks appeared reluctant to lend money to support exports of coal plants for fear that they would turn into stranded assets (Downie and Hughes 2020).

Nor did aggressive efforts to export nuclear technology proceed smoothly. In 2006, Toshiba spent over $5 billion to acquire Westinghouse's nuclear power business. The next year Mitsubishi Heavy Industries formed a joint venture with the French nuclear firm Areva, while in 2012 Hitachi bought Britain's Horizon Nuclear Power. The Japanese companies embarked on five projects to build nuclear power plants in Europe, the Middle East and Asia. By 2019, however, delays, excessive costs, and the aftermath of the Fukushima nuclear disaster led all five to be canceled or frozen (*Nikkei Asia*, January 11, 2019). The Japanese companies then shifted attention to provision of parts and services to existing nuclear plants.

Other efforts to export large infrastructure projects struggled to cut costs, achieve localization, and overcome domestic political obstacles, as well as to match fierce competition from German, French, Chinese, and South Korean companies. Japan's famous shinkansen bullet trains achieved some successes, notably providing 70 percent of Taiwan's high-speed speed rail system and building a 508 kilometer line in India between Mumbai and Ahmedabad, 80 percent funded by a soft loan from the Japan International Cooperation Agency (JICA), in return for Indian agreement to restrict procurement to Japanese firms (Hood 2007, Grey 2017). Many other shinkansen projects, however, have been mired in disappointment, including loss to China (Indonesia), cancelation (Malaysia-Singapore), and seemingly endless delay and uncertainty (Thailand, Vietnam, Texas). Hitachi and other Japanese rail companies have found some moderate success, however, in supplying trains and signaling equipment to existing railways in Spain, the United Kingdom, and the United States, and in supplying or managing subway systems (see e.g. *Nikkei Asia* August 16, 2019).

Perhaps the most painful double-duty export failure was the loss of a giant project to supply submarines to Australia (Kelly, Altmeyer, and Packham 2016, Sheftalovich 2021). Soon after Abe Shinzo returned as prime minister in 2012, Japan appeared to have wrapped up a deal to sell Australia twelve diesel submarines worth tens of billions of dollars. However, after a change of partisan control in Australia, France won the order with promises of local production in South Australia and significant technology transfer, promises the Japanese companies seemed unwilling to make or unaware that they needed to match. After another change in leadership, and complaints about the terms and progress of the French deal, Australia then abrogated the agreement and arranged to acquire nuclear submarine technology from the United States and the United Kingdom, profoundly reshaping the strategic map of the Asia-Pacific.

Semiconductors: From Global Triumph to Bailouts to Economic Security

No industry displays the transformation in Japanese industrial policy more starkly than semiconductors. A triumph in the 1970s and 1980s – with considerable help from the government – by the 2000s, METI scrambled to save the remnants of a shattered industry, with at best mixed results. Then in the 2020s, the government began pouring massive sums into semiconductors in the name of national security. If the resulting wave of investments relied too heavily on government subsidies to be considered a clear commercial success, they seemed sufficiently positive in technological and geopolitical terms to justify the government's efforts, at least for a time.

Few products are more essential to advanced economies (and militaries) than semiconductors, the embodied intelligence powering computers, telecommunications, and a myriad of commercial and consumer products. In the 1970s and 1980s, most design and production of semiconductors was integrated. Japanese companies, with their teams of experienced engineers working closely with suppliers, attained low costs through high yields, moved rapidly from one generation of products to the next, and – aided by a supportive industrial policy – achieved a dominant position in the world semiconductor market.

In the 1990s, however, the cost of building increasingly complex fabrication plants spiraled upward. Only the largest producers sold enough output to make full use of their production capacity. American companies specialized in software and design, and outsourced production to contract manufacturers, especially Taiwan Semiconductor Manufacturing Company. TSMC became the world's first "pure fab": by promising not to produce its own designs or create its own brand, TSMC was able to spread the cost of fabrication over many clients, who could be sure that their intellectual property would be secure. South Korean semiconductor manufacturers, led by Samsung, specialized in DRAM memory chips, in which they made huge investments. Japan was left with too many companies producing similar products, all struggling to invest in expensive new plants.

Corporate pride and the permanent employment system made Japanese companies reluctant to merge, so METI stepped in to urge and support corporate restructuring. First to move was the memory sector. NEC and Hitachi merged their DRAM operations in 1999 to form Elpida Memory, which then absorbed the memory division of Mitsubishi Electric. In 2009, amid the global financial crisis, Elpida received 300 billion yen (then worth a little over three billion dollars) from the Japanese government, but by 2012 the surge of the yen to an all-time high of less than 80 yen to the dollar and a decline in the always-volatile price of DRAMs pushed Elpida into bankruptcy. In 2013 it was acquired by Micron Technology of the United States (*Asahi* December 29, 2021).

Marginally more successful was the case of Renesas, a maker of micro-controllers and a leading supplier to the automobile industry. Renesas was formed in 2003 by the merger of non-DRAM chip divisions of Hitachi and Mitsubishi. In 2010 Renesas absorbed NEC Electronics. But the Fukushima nuclear disaster of 2011, the sharp appreciation of the yen, and intensifying global competition pushed to Renesas to the wall. METI then took action. In 2009, amidst the shock of the global financial crisis, METI had drafted an industrial competitiveness law creating a public-private fund called the Innovation Network Corporation of Japan (INCJ) to support high-risk ventures and restructure troubled companies. About 300 billion yen in capital, the vast majority of it from the government's Fiscal Investment and Loan Program, supported roughly six times as much in government loan guarantees. Well over half of lending was devoted not to innovative start-ups but to corporate reorganizations of struggling firms (*Nikkei Asia*, August 10, 2017). INCJ rescued cash-strapped Renesas in 2013 with an investment of 138 billion yen (then about $1.4 billion) and received a 69 percent ownership stake (INCJ 2018). The company's financial condition improved sharply over the next couple of years and INCJ gradually sold stock until its ownership share declined to 32 percent. Renesas's revenues, however, stagnated in the decade following the bailout.

The last sector to consolidate was flat panel displays, a technology closely related to semiconductors. In 2011, as Japanese makers of displays struggled to keep up with South Korean and Chinese rivals, METI organized a rescue. Sony, Toshiba, and Hitachi merged their divisions producing small-sized to medium-sized LCD panels into Japan Display, an "all-Japan" joint venture with the INCJ, which contributed 70 percent of the capital.

Japan Display flourished for a couple of years. However, JDI's major client was Apple, and when sales of Apple's iPhone softened and JDI's investments in new technology failed to keep up with South Korean and Chinese competitors, the company fell into the red. Critics assailed the company's slow, hydra-headed decision-making process (companies, JDI, INCJ, METI). Even after selling the company off to private investors in 2020, the red ink continued (*Asahi* May 15, 2022).

As Section 2 noted, until recently, Japanese government expenditures on promotion of industrial technology have been surprisingly modest, contrasting sharply with the emphasis placed on energy. Under pressure from the United States to help counter China and reduce reliance on Taiwan, however, Japan shifted to a much more aggressive stance, with a particular emphasis on semiconductors – despite the disappointing record of recent years.

In accordance with the 2022 law on economic security introduced in Section 1, an expert panel identified twenty specific products both essential for national survival and excessively dependent on potentially unreliable external suppliers (Cabinet Secretariat 2022b). Semiconductors attracted the greatest attention and the biggest subsidies.

Even before formal identification of critical technologies, the government began subsidizing investments in domestic production facilities by foreign semiconductor companies. This marked a major break with the traditional practice of concentrating support on domestic firms. The support for foreign investment in semiconductors focused on companies from Taiwan and the United States, and even then, there was some unease about the technological value of the investments and the companies' likely loyalty in the event of an economic crisis.

The second supplementary budget bill for 2022 provided ¥1,305 billion (about $9.3 billion at $1 = ¥140) for semiconductor development by private firms and AIST, including

- ¥450 billion toward bringing production hubs for advanced chips to Japan
- ¥485 billion for research collaboration with the U.S. on the development of next-generation semiconductors for telecommunications.
- ¥370 billion for securing materials essential for strengthening semiconductor supply chains (*Nikkei Asia* November 6, 2022); (Yasuda 2021, METI 2022c). The supplementary budgets from 2020 to 2023 also supported numerous cooperative semiconductor projects at Japanese universities (Uno 2022).

The first and biggest subsidy involved Taiwan Semiconductor Manufacturing Company's proposed investment in a joint venture with Sony and leading Toyota supplier Denso to build a factory to produce logic chips in Kumamoto prefecture on the southern island of Kyushu. The government offered subsidies of up to ¥476 billion ($3.5 billion), 40 percent of the total construction cost, plus ¥19 billion ($140 million) for a TSMC research center in Tsukuba. A second set of subsidies totaling over $1.5 billion was awarded to a joint venture between Kioxia, a spinoff from Toshiba, and the American firm Western Digital to build an advanced flash memory plant (Kioxia 2024). Similarly, Micron Technology received a subsidy of ¥46.5 billion to upgrade the former Elpida memory plant in Hiroshima (*Nikkei* September 30, 2022). Overall, Japan's leading business newspaper reported that Japanese semiconductor firms were planning to invest over $30 billion through 2029, with an average subsidy rate of 30 percent (*Nikkei* July 8, 2024).

All in all, this represented the most ambitious and muscular attempt at industrial promotion in decades. At the same time, it raised old dilemmas of cooperation and leadership highlighted by Callon (1995) back at the peak of the financial bubble: would Japanese companies commit their best researchers and greatest financial efforts to cooperative ventures, or save their resources for proprietary projects? A new problem noted above was the scale of investment required for modern chip fabrication plants. After decades of domestic decline of both semiconductors and the downstream industries that consumed them, did Japanese companies have the capacity and sheer audacity to invest continuously at the scale and speed required to compete globally?

These concerns came to the fore when eight leading Japanese companies, including Toyota, NTT, and Sony, announced the founding of a joint company to develop next-generation logic chips, with help in research and development from IBM. METI promised to provide the optimistically-named Rapidus with ¥70 billion in initial funding. An *Asahi Shinbun* editorial laid out the case against Rapidus:

> The eight companies that came together for the undertaking only managed to cough up 7.3 billion yen in total … This makes it hard to assess which company will take the leadership role and responsibility for the venture. It appears the companies provided money only as a goodwill gesture for government policymakers and Liberal Democratic Party politicians who harbor dreams of making Japan the semiconductor powerhouse it once was. [The companies] likely are less than enthusiastic about the project because they do not see any realistic use of the envisioned device in Japan. The cutting-edge logic chips the new company is expected to develop will be designed mainly for personal computers and smartphones. But large-scale domestic manufacturing facilities for these products no longer exist in Japan. The industry ministry asserts that the semiconductor devices will be needed for fully self-driving vehicles in the future. But automobiles generally use tested and proven older-generation chips as priority is placed on safety in car manufacturing. (*Asahi*, November 17, 2022; see also *Nikkei*, November 12, 2022)

Despite these warnings, METI doubled down on its efforts to use Rapidus to revive cutting-edge semiconductor production in Japan. In April 2024, the government approved additional subsidies of up to 590 billion yen (about $3.89 billion) to fund construction of a plant to produce semiconductors with line widths of just two nanometers by 2027 (CNBC April 2, 2024).

This initial wave of investment by foreign and Japanese firms showed some positive results. Thanks to the geographic and cultural propinquity of Japan and Taiwan, Japan's relatively loose regulations on land and labor, and the opportunity to rekindle the remnants of Japan's once-impressive supply chain of semiconductor parts and materials, TSMC's first fabrication plant in Kumamoto came on line in February 2024, years before the first factories from TSMC's $40 billion investment in Arizona. TSMC's new factories in Japan, the United States, and Germany began to alleviate some of policymakers' fears about the concentration of advanced semiconductor production in Taiwan, with its vulnerability to Chinese attack or coercion (*New York Times,* May 9, 2024).

Yet serious doubts about the long-run viability of Japan's semiconductor policy remained. Given the immense complexity and high degree of specialization in the global semiconductor industry, consulting companies and industry executives questioned the feasibility of individual and even collective efforts to decouple supply networks: "So-called supply chain resilience has become a central aim of policy. But such resilience is a myth." Morris Chang, the founder of TSMC, warned the United States (and by extension Japan and other countries) saying, "Even after you spend hundreds of billions of dollars, you will still find the supply chain to be incomplete, and you will find that it will be very high cost, much higher cost than what you currently have" (*Nikkei Asia* July 27, 2022).

Daunting Tasks, Limited Resources, and Few Successes

The record of Japanese industrial policy after the early 1980s is at best mixed and it is difficult to identify striking successes. As noted above, this reflects the limitations of both Japanese industry and of government policy. A possible exception is semiconductors. Since 2020, when the critical measure of success shifted to national security, arguably policy toward semiconductors has succeeding in reviving a crucial industry, but the cost has been high and may not be sustainable. If promotion of the defense and space industries contributed to technological "spin-offs" in the United States in the 1960s, while in later decades, Japan was able to "spin on" some commercial technologies to defense uses (Samuels 1994), it is not clear how advanced semiconductor production can contribute to national security if it is not grounded in a commercially competitive electronics industry.

6 The Transformation of Industrial Policy in Japan's Neighbors

The arc of development of the industrial policies of Japan's northeast Asian neighbors bears some important similarities to that of Japan. South Korea, Taiwan, and China were all influenced by Japanese colonialism, trade and investment, and all were deeply impressed by Japan's successful example of development. All three experienced extended periods of mobilization to fight civil wars and invasion. All (with the partial exception of China until the early 1990s) depended heavily upon imports of natural resources, particularly oil. In all three, the government actively promoted industrial catchup through industrial policy. All three featured financial systems dominated by banks owned or tightly regulated by the government, and restricted imports and inward foreign investment through the 1980s and beyond. All gradually moved from protectionist trade policies and strong state intervention to liberalization and globalization, amid continuing concern about dependence on an often-threatening external environment.

Yet the shift in emphasis from development to national security has been less abrupt, because industrial policy in Japan's neighbors has always been tightly linked to national security. This is especially true of China. Where Taiwan and South Korea operate under the American defense and technological umbrella, China is a direct rival. Partly as a consequence, where top-down industrial planning and reliance on state-owned enterprises has sharply declined in South Korea and Taiwan, it remains important in China.

South Korea and Taiwan

Of the three countries, South Korea modeled itself most closely upon Japanese policy, yet a markedly different style of industrial policy emerged. Through the late 1980s, South Korea's military-dominated government held periodic presidential elections but no local elections. The ruling party depended on financial contributions from big business in return for protection against foreign capital and labor unions. Not surprisingly, support for small-sized and medium-sized enterprises and local economies was less prominent than in Japan. South Korea's presidents were much more prone to exert top-down rule from the "Blue House" and regularly shook up the central bureaucracy, leaving South Korea without a stable counterpart to MITI. Constrained by a much smaller, poorer domestic market than that of Japan and by an even greater paucity of natural resources, South Korean policymakers abandoned their initial preference for autarky and ended up relying on cheap labor to produce standardized industrial products for export. Intent upon shoring up their legitimacy and political support through economic success, and facing a credible national security threat from an initially more industrialized North Korean regime, the South Korean government adopted an aggressive policy style and shoveled bank loans to firms that proved themselves capable of building huge factories and competing on foreign markets, peaking with the Heavy and Chemical Industries (HCI) drive of the 1980s (Choi and Levchenko 2021).

The result was an industrial structure dominated by a small number of huge conglomerates called *chaebol*. As the conglomerates matured and engaged in more capital and technology-intensive production, developed global brands such as Samsung, LG, and Hyundai, and invested abroad, they became increasingly independent of government, particularly after democratization and the privatization of banking in the 1980s and 1990s. While political concerns over economic inequality and the weak position of small firms grew, South Korean conglomerates were still able to bend policy to fit their strategies because of their centrality to economic performance and because they staff some of South Korea's major institutions, including ministries and agencies, presidential committees, and public–private consultative councils. Even left-wing parties that campaigned against the conglomerates during elections found themselves forced to cooperate when they took power (Kang and Jo 2021).

Business representation is more concentrated and direct than in Japan. The Federation of Korean Industries (FKI) operates essentially as a club of the leading conglomerates. Similarly, business association are dominated by the big business groups. The Korean Automobile Manufacturers Association, for example, has just six member firms, of which Hyundai-Kia is completely dominant. Electronics is somewhat more diverse, but it is still dominated by just two-and-a-half firms: Samsung, LG, and SK Hynix. Since democratization, small- and medium-sized firms receive much more political sympathy, but they are harder to organize and economically less consequential, so when push comes to shove, industrial policy favors the conglomerates (Kang and Jo 2021).

Though it patterned itself less directly on Japan than South Korea did, Taiwan, with its balance of large, medium and small firms, came to resemble Japan more closely, albeit in a smaller and weaker form. Taiwan did not conduct national elections until the 1990s, but did have local elections, so it was much less beholden to big business and more attuned to local concerns and the interests of small firms. The ruling Kuomintang (KMT) party, with its strong "quasi-Leninist" party organization inherited from its days on mainland China, was far more adept than South Korea's military regime at social control and electoral manipulation. The KMT "party-state" took over rich assets inherited from the Japanese colonial regime to build a significant (but gradually declining) state-owned sector that provided many upstream products such as petrochemicals and steel to private firms both large and small that engaged in labor-intensive downstream processing and assembly, mostly for export. The disastrous experience of hyperinflation on mainland China in the 1940s and the huge ethnic Chinese diaspora in Hong Kong and Southeast Asia made Taiwan more vulnerable to inflation and capital flight, so it was much more restrained in allocation of capital and macroeconomic policy than was South Korea.

The Ten Major Construction Projects of the late 1970s did pour resources into state-owned steel, machinery, and shipbuilding operations, but the projects were more restrained than the HCI Drive in South Korea, and more oriented to building infrastructure. After the second oil shock in 1979, the government quickly switched attention from heavy industry to high technology, beefing up the Industrial Technology Research Institute (ITRI) and the Science-Based Industrial Park in Hsinchu, just south of Taipei. ITRI soon spun off semiconductor start-ups, led by Taiwan Semiconductor Manufacturing Company (TSMC), which grew into the world's largest contract manufacturer of semiconductor chips, and provided technical support to electronics companies (Tung 2001). Instead of trying to compete directly with foreign firms, as South Korean companies such as Hyundai did in autos and Samsung in electronics, Taiwanese companies led by Foxconn, the world's biggest contract electronics manufacturer, typically worked as suppliers to foreign giants such as Apple and Dell.

By the 1990s, large firms and business groups gradually gained in prominence but they remained constrained (Amsden and Chu 2003). Labor-intensive operations moved to China and Southeast Asia, especially after "reform and opening" in China and revaluation of the New Taiwan Dollar. As in South Korea, Taiwanese companies gradually moved into capital and skill-intensive industries and the increasingly liberalized financial sector. Taiwan became the world leader in semiconductor production. But there was still a gap with South Korea: Taiwanese companies were smaller and less independent than the South Korean chaebol, rarely sold products under their own brands, and devoted a somewhat smaller share of GDP to research and development (especially basic research) than the South Koreans (though they surpassed the Japanese) (OECD).

Taiwan resembles Japan in having broad peak and industry associations. Industrial policy is focused around the Ministry of Economic Affairs and the Industrial Technology Research Institute, which are in close contact with industry associations. The Ministry of Defense's National Chungshan Institute of Science and Technology assumes primary responsibility for defense technology, but it also occasionally works with private firms on dual-use technology such as air bags (based on expertise in explosives) and radar.

Like South Korea, Taiwan has experienced democratization and repeated partisan turnover. With the notable exception of nuclear power, however, industrial policy has not been a particularly contentious issue. Government personnel in both countries are more technocratic and less confined in ministerial silos than in Japan – in that sense, they are perhaps more similar to elite bureaucrats in France or Britain. Most technocrats serve a stint in the military and often go to the United States for graduate training before joining ministries. They tend to be older and have a less acute sense of belonging to a ministry cohort. Sometimes they move to other ministries. Many have risen to become minister at the various iterations of the Ministry of Finance and Economy (MOFE) in South Korea, or the Ministry of Economic Affairs (MOEA) in Taiwan, without ever becoming career politicians or serving in the legislature. Especially in South Korea, officials appointed by the president sometimes "parachute" directly into high-level positions in ministries and agencies (Lee and Kim 2018).

Today, economic planning and overall coordination are far less prominent than in the heyday of South Korea's Economic Planning Board (EPB) and Taiwan's Council for Economic Planning and Development (CEPD) from the 1960s to the early 1990s. However, both countries still engage in some targeting of strategic industries and display considerable continuity in economic ministries and their associated technological support agencies (Intarakumnerd 2011). In some areas, such as domestic and international industrial standards, and support for smaller enterprises in joining global production networks, the role of the state in promoting industrial coordination has actually grown (Chu 2021). Both governments still maintain significant influence over funding. In South Korea, even as preferential lending has declined, the government has sharply increased provision of trade insurance and credit guarantees (Lee and Kim 2018). Both South Korea and Taiwan have witnessed huge increases in spending on R&D since the early 1990s. Most is still privately funded, as in Japan, but some of it is in response to government initiatives, and South Korean government R&D expenditures as a share of GDP have more than doubled in recent years (Hourihan and Zimmermann 2022).

Like Japan, South Korea and Taiwan depend heavily on imported energy but have remained reluctant to commit fully to renewable energy. South Korea, like Japan, has strongly favored nuclear power over renewables and has viewed nuclear power as a potential export industry, though nuclear policy has become been more subject to partisan contestation (*Nikkei Asia* December 2, 2022). South Korea's leading automaker Hyundai is following Toyota on hydrogen as in everything else and may even be pulling ahead.

Taiwan, where nuclear policy has been a key partisan dispute since the formation of the Democratic Progressive Party in 1986, has never aspired to export nuclear technology. It *has* attempted to turn wind power into an export industry, even at the cost of discouraging foreign investment and delaying deployment, despite extreme reliance on imported energy and fear of Chinese blockades (Ferry 2020).

As in Japan, globalization, democratization, and economic catchup have weakened the role of industrial policy in South Korea and Taiwan. Industrial policy continues, and each new administration announces new favored industries in an attempt to diversify and break into more profitable areas, but no big breakthroughs have been achieved, and both remain weak in software and biotechnology (Wong 2011, Fuller 2022). Yet the recency of industrial catchup, and an even stronger sense of vulnerability in the face of more powerful and (in the case of China and North Korea) closer and more hostile neighbors, has sustained "developmental will" more acutely among both the elite and the voting public. This is especially true in South Korea, which has less conflict over its identity in the region and in the global political economy (Kim and Thurbon 2015).

China

Industrial policy in China has been deeply shaped by threats to security, including revolution, civil war, the Korean War, border tensions with the Soviet Union and India, and pressure from the United States (Feigenbaum 2003). After the victory of the communist revolution in 1949, a Leninist party presided over a planned economy with an industrial sector dominated by state-owned enterprises and oriented to strengthening national defense. Yet China's industrial structure and pattern of government–business relations were not simply Stalinist, but were complicated by the country's size, diversity, and revolutionary heritage of local initiative. Most "state-owned" firms were actually owned and sponsored by municipal and provincial governments. After "reform and opening" began in 1979, and especially after China joined the WTO in 2001, many private firms emerged. Foreign investment, often with vigorous promotion from local governments, also poured in, at first aiming at sales in the domestic market, but increasingly making China the workshop to the world.

Yet despite the great economic success of the opening to domestic and foreign capital, the communist party has grown uneasy at the growth in business power and economic inequality. China still has far more policy tools than does Japan, though it finds it difficult to coordinate policy across levels and sectors of government. China still employs controls over movement of capital and foreign exchange. The state still owns the largest banks. Protection against imports of goods and investment has been reduced but by no means eliminated. The party under Xi Jinping caused the state to "strike back," strengthening the state-owned sector and reining in private firms, particularly internet giants such as Alibaba, Tencent, and Baidu (Lardy 2019, Pearson, Rithmire, and Tsai 2023).

The government strove, with some success, to reduce reliance on foreign technology, most famously in the *Made in China 2025* plan (State Council 2015, Zenglein and Holzmann 2019). China's research funding system is often criticized and remains weak in some areas, such as medicine and bio-sciences. Yet Chinese research is extremely impressive in many areas basic to industry and manufacturing, such as chemistry and engineering, as demonstrated by skyrocketing production of patents and "top 1% most-cited" international journal articles in science, mathematics, and engineering (Naughton 2018: 363–394, Hourihan and Zimmermann 2022).

Organizationally, China's industrial policy machinery is complex and sometimes conflictual, but relatively stable. The key agents driving industrial policy are still the National Development and Reform Commission (NDRC), the descendant of socialist planning commissions; the State Council's Development Research Center, which brings a stronger market orientation; and the Ministry of Industry and Information Technology (MIIT). The State-owned Assets Supervision and Administration Commission of the State Council (SASAC) also plays an important part, as do the local analogs of all three, as well as the party itself, and its leadership small groups. As China moved away from socialist planning and embarked on reform and opening in the 1980s and 1990s it borrowed the concept of industrial policy and industrial visions from Japan and Germany – as seen most famously in *Made in China 2025* and industrial plans for automobiles and semiconductors – but the resultant documents were often at least as vacuous as their Japanese counterparts (Fuller 2019, Doner, Noble, and Ravenhill 2021).

The Communist Party exercises tight control over careers at government agencies and centrally owned SOEs but career management is considerably looser at local agencies, local SOEs, and especially at private firms, though occasional party interventions, as at privately-owned platform giants such as Alibaba or Tencent, can be disconcerting.

China, of course, has not experienced democratization, and is marked by chronic tension between dynamic private firms and political control by the party-state. Kennedy (2005) finds that Chinese industry associations are varied and active, and while not autonomous, they are neither exclusive nor hierarchical. Looking at the manufacture and sales of automobiles, Doner et al. (2021) also find a modest amount of pluralism and some increase in organizational capacity, but see associations as still firmly under the control of the party. Recent years have seen some lobbying by individual firms, especially large private companies in the electronics and information industries, including through the media and quasi-representative bodies in the state and party, but the party center has brought them sharply to heel (McGregor 2021). Chinese industrial policy is the product of the central and local party-states. Industry associations and private firms play a distinctly secondary role.

When it comes to energy, China shares many similarities with its northeast Asian neighbors, including high population density, heavy reliance on imported energy, interest in hydrogen, and tendency to view energy policy as industrial policy. It differs from them, however, in having extensive endowments of coal and rare earths and other critical minerals, along with modest deposits of oil and gas. China has adopted an "all of the above" policy of aggressively promoting investment in all forms of energy, including renewables, hydrogen, and nuclear, all while continuing to rely on coal in the meantime (Jiang, Gao, and Geall 2022). China treats virtually all energy technologies as potential export industries. It has become a major player in nuclear power and a global leader in renewable energy and processing of rare earths.

China's industrial policy has had some success in promoting moves from assembly to engineering to innovation and branding, as seen for example, in an outpouring of electric and hydrogen vehicles, some of which boast sophisticated designs and software that can credibly compete with Tesla. Yet progress is slowing amidst a political crackdown on the private sector and ever-increasing tensions with the United States over trade and technology. China's big push to domesticate design and production of advanced semiconductors has achieved limited success so far and faces increasing pressure from the US (Fuller 2021).

The Future of Industrial Policy in Japan's Neighbors

In South Korea and Taiwan, economic globalization, political change, administrative reform, and demographic pressures have narrowed the scope and impact of once formidable developmental states, yet much of the industrial policy apparatus remains in place amid concerns about increasing reliance on imported energy and technology (cf. Noble 2017). China looks somewhat different, with its huge market, continued reliance on oligopolistic state-owned enterprise groups, and determination to break through American-led technology blockades. But China still relies excessively on state-directed investment, especially in industry, real estate, and infrastructure, and on exports to an increasingly wary world. Household consumption is anemic, in part due to an inadequate social safety net. Without much more rapid growth of the service sector, white-collar employment is likely to remain weak. In the eyes of the public, and even some policymakers, industrial policy may come to seem as much an obstacle as a success.

7 Conclusion

In the last decade or so, an unexpected resurgence of industrial policy has occurred in Japan. In part, this reflects a change in Japan's economic environment. From the late 1980s until around 2010, industrial policy seemed increasingly peripheral. Picking promising sectors for promotion became more difficult as Japanese firms reached world technology frontiers. Where Japanese firms once produced at home for both the domestic and export markets, increasingly they engaged in overseas foreign investment, largely beyond the reach of Japanese protection and promotion. Financial liberalization and low interest rates rendered policy loans increasingly irrelevant. Economic policy focused fewer resources on technology development in specific industries and more on "horizontal" policies designed to enhance the efficiency and flexibility of the overall economy, such as improving corporate governance, loosening restrictions on start-ups, and strengthening protection of intellectual property rights. Within the energy sector, policy choices seemed settled, even banal: nuclear power provided an increasingly large share of electricity generation, displacing first coal and then LNG, while solar power, though still accounting for only a tiny share of overall generation, made rapid technical and economic progress, thanks mostly to leadership by Japanese electronics companies.

The Perceived Need for Industrial Rejuvenation

By the late 2000s, however, Japanese firms had suffered an alarming decline in competitive position and global market share. Japan's East Asian rivals came to challenge Japan in sophisticated manufacturing, including production of semiconductors and solar panels, and proved more innovative in software and communications; all three moved more quickly to embrace e-commerce, e-government, and the transition to a cashless society. South Korea and Taiwan matched Japan's wages and R&D spending as a share of GDP, while China completely surpassed Japan in production of international journal articles in science and engineering. Meanwhile, a shift in economic activity from manufacturing to design, software, and web services, led by American companies such as Google, Amazon, Facebook and Apple, meant that Japanese companies were no longer assured of a place "at the technology frontier."

The global financial crisis of 2007–09 and the nearly simultaneous "rise of China" also led to a major change in the intellectual environment. Even the

World Bank and the IMF came to admit that there was a significant role for industrial policy in enhancing information, coordination, diffusion, and capacity building as well as in ameliorating the strains that outsourcing and globalization placed on labor markets and declining regions.

Compounding these economic and intellectual changes was an unsettling deterioration in the security environment surrounding Japan, including missile threats from North Korea and a precipitous rise in the military capabilities of China. Particularly worrisome was the increase in territorial disputes, including conflicts over the Senkaku/Diaoyudao Islands and the potential oil and gas reserves surrounding them; the demarcation of the central line between China and Japan in the East China Sea, site of significant gas reserves; China's expansive claims to the South China Sea, with its energy resources, fishing activities, and busy maritime shipping; and above all, China's refusal to renounce the use of force in pursuit of its claims to sovereignty over Taiwan.

The increasing pressures on Japan's economic and security environment in the 2010s were refracted through the centralization of power in the cabinet and prime minister's office, with which METI managed to retain close connections. The Japanese government mounted a vigorous industrial policy response. It engaged in export initiatives linked to diplomacy and security, including submarines and infrastructure such as shinkansen bullet trains, coal power stations, and nuclear power plants. It increased support for aviation (both civilian and fighter jets) and promoted the use of hydrogen and ammonia as crucial energy carriers and storage media for use in automobiles, steel, electricity generation, and other industries. Once the shock of the Fukushima meltdown receded and the new nuclear inspection system was in place, the government resumed efforts to promote nuclear power, including restarting and allowing license extensions for existing reactors, building new reactors on existing sites, and supporting development of next generation reactors. The government made strenuous efforts to promote the revival of production of semiconductors and other strategic materials and technologies, supported by huge supplemental budgets from 2020 to 2023, and passed a wide-ranging economic security law in 2022.

Japan thus combined a strong *demand* for industrial policy from political leaders and the business community with a continuing capacity to *supply* industrial policy by METI and other ministries, under the direction of the LDP and the Cabinet, that could still deploy significant human, financial, and organizational resources.

The revival of industrial policy amid heightened security concerns, particularly responding to the rise of Chinese military power, is not limited to Japan, of course. Nor is increasing popular disillusionment with the expansion of outsourcing and economic globalization. Governments across Asia, Australia,

North America, and Europe are attempting to craft industrial strategies to strengthen indigenous capabilities and reduce dependence on imports of vital products (Benson and Mouradian 2023). For better or worse, however, Japan displays more institutional and policy continuity and deeper government–business relations then most other countries.

A Dearth of Success Stories

Yet Japan has confronted a vexing dilemma. Despite the sense of urgency and the flurry of action, as of the mid-2020s, it is difficult to point to unambiguous cases of successful industrial policies. Apart from supplying part of Taiwan's high-speed rail system, few of the efforts to export transportation and energy infrastructure led to completed projects, while the attempt to sell submarines to Australia ended in ignominious rejection. At the end of 2022, the Japanese government did reach an agreement with Italy and the United Kingdom to co-develop a next-generation fighter aircraft but the results of the project would not be visible until 2035 at the earliest. In early 2023, Mitsubishi Heavy Industries finally pulled the plug on development of its regional jet. Promotion of hydrogen and ammonia as energy carriers also faces tough going. Even with lavish subsidies, sales of hydrogen fuel cell cars have ignominiously stalled. Efforts to promote the use of hydrogen in steel production and electricity generation continue, but face formidable challenges to cut costs, expand fuel supply, and curb emissions of pollution. Prospects for significant expansion of nuclear power remain uncertain at best. Several attempts in the 2010s to bail out semiconductor companies ended in failure. Even with major subsidies in the early 2020s, and some initial success in reviving semiconductor production and supply chains, it remains unclear if Japanese producers will be willing and able to sustain the massive investments required to remain competitive on the international market.

Industrial Policy Challenges

Despite the scarcity of heartening success stories, widespread perceptions of economic and security vulnerability suggest that industrial policy is unlikely simply to disappear. It will, however, have to confront a number of pressing challenges.

Funding and Coordination

If Japanese industrial policy is to succeed in strengthening industries with important implications for national security, it cannot rely solely on cooperation with the private sector but will need to engage in greater public investment. The government will need to enhance funding for basic R&D

infrastructure and training and do more to ensure the long-term employment of PhDs in science and technology fields, particularly in software and data science, which are not only important industries in their own right but also increasingly crucial to the success of the manufacturing industries that have been the traditional objects of industrial policy. Biotechnology, for example, regularly features in lists of industrial policy initiatives, yet Japan's global position in life sciences has declined drastically since the 1990s as a result of the government's failure to invest adequately in basic research and its short-sighted insistence on continually squeezing prices of innovative new drugs. Similarly, Japan will have a hard time catching up with China and the United States in the bourgeoning fields of artificial intelligence (AI) and robotics without greater investment in Japan's computing infrastructure.

Balancing Coordination and Innovation

Japanese industrial policy has tended to focus on coordination of interests to strengthen Japan's position in production of such integrated products as automobiles, aircraft, and nuclear power plants, and in organizing complex supply networks, such as those for semiconductor fabrication or distribution of hydrogen. This tendency is exacerbated by the continuity and reluctance to take risk engendered by the "silo"-like personnel system of METI and other ministries. METI is sensitive to the need to avoid cutting off technological diversity, as seen in its initial support for both battery and hydrogen vehicles, but its inclination to coordinate and back the priorities of dominant mainstream firms militates against taking risky bets on new technologies and start-up firms. Japan may need to take some hints from America's Defense Advanced Research Projects Agency (DARPA), which has achieved impressive results by delegating authority to specialist project managers aiming to make breakthroughs in a strictly limited time period (Bonvillian, Van Atta, and Windham 2019).

The government will have to find ways to encourage firms to introduce greater flexibility and higher mobility into labor markets for scientists and engineers. New startups will not appear and flourish if they cannot hire experienced scientist and engineers. Yet it is crucial to introduce employment reforms and incentives without creating excessive insecurity and engendering a social backlash. Part of the solution will probably include increasing immigration and creating denser networks with overseas researchers. The government may also need to consider increasing the direct employment of scientists and engineers to bring Japan up to OECD averages. Any of these initiatives will require greater coordination among the cabinet and related ministries, including METI, MEXT (the Ministry of Education, Culture, Sports, Science and Technology), and the

Ministry of Justice. Enhancing coordination, in turn, will require sustained political leadership.

Balancing Breadth with Focus in an Era of Limits and Competing Priorities

In the name of enhancing economic security, METI and the Japanese government have listed a dizzying array of industries for possible promotion and protection, including semiconductors, aviation, batteries, critical minerals, software, biotechnology, and more. The human and financial resources necessary to promote these industries are limited and face competing priorities. Already plagued with massive budget deficits, the Japanese government has committed to spending more to provide pensions and health care for an aging society; double defense spending; support aging and declining regional economies; shield consumers from surging prices of imported food and energy; and encourage increased fertility. So far, the government has resorted to compiling extraordinarily large supplemental budgets. Will it repeat that pattern in coming years? Or expand the share of industrial policy in regular current account budgets despite all the competing priorities? The government will find it difficult to sustain public support for enhanced expenditures on economic security if it cannot point to clearer success stories than have appeared so far. If industrial policy is unlikely to disappear completely as long as Japan feels vulnerable to external threats and to pressure from the United States, it may well fade in scope and ambition.

Balancing the United States, China, and the Global Trading System

As Japanese corporations have increasingly shifted production abroad, policymakers have come to support and even exert leadership in the global trade and investment regime. They also must deal, however, with rising protectionism and the possible evolution of competing supply chains oriented to the United States and China, respectively. Japan is already under considerable pressure from the United States to reduce trade with China. At the same time, Japan needs to stay connected with market demand, especially Chinese and Asian demand, which is much more important to Japan and its Asian allies and partners than to the United States. Japan also needs to navigate among the sometimes-competing, sometimes-complementary industrial policies of Europe, the United States, and other partners such as Australia. In the case of the next-generation fighter jet, for example, Japan chose to reject the United States, which "black-boxes" much of the technology in its joint development projects, in favor of a more open and balanced alliance with Britain and Italy.

If Japan is to reduce reliance on Chinese value chains, industrial policy will have to craft feasible and sustainable alternatives. This may prove difficult. In the critical case of manufacturing cutting-edge semiconductors, for example, Japan and the United States have much higher production costs than Taiwan and South Korea, and they no longer produce many products that require chips with the narrowest circuit widths. Even if Japanese companies succeed in catching up with South Korea and Taiwan, they may find it difficult to sustain succeeding generations of massive investments.

Reducing reliance on China for the rare earths and other critical materials that are indispensable for the production of missiles, wind turbines, electric cars, and many other vital products is likely to prove equally challenging. Japanese experts stress that China has ignored severe environmental externalities to build up a near monopoly in mining (first at home and then increasingly through investment in mining projects overseas), which it has allegedly used as a political tool, most notably after the Senkaku boat collision incident of 2010. To be sure, Chinese efforts to exploit monopoly power can easily backfire, as consumers of rare earths seek to diversify and find more reliable suppliers, but Japanese efforts to devise an effective response are still likely to prove complicated and expensive. Moreover, less recognized is that China has built a massive lead in the technology and capital equipment required to process rare earths. The Japanese government will need to coordinate carefully with Japanese firms and with such allies as the United States, Australia, and Canada, all while trying to maintain stable commercial relations with China, which will maintain a dominant position in rare earth processing for the foreseeable future.

Finally, the United States and Japan have to balance national security concerns about Chinese-centered trade networks with maintenance of an open global trading system. Under the Trump and Biden administrations, the United States hobbled and bypassed the World Trade Organization; withdrew from the proposed Trans-Pacific Partnership (TPP); rejected its successor, the Comprehensive and Progressive Agreement for Trans-Pacific Partnership (CPTPP or TPP-11); and structured industrial policies for automobiles and semiconductors so as to exclude imports, investment, and even technology from China, creating dilemmas for Japanese, South Korean, and Taiwanese firms that were highly dependent on inputs from China. These moves exacted significant collateral damage on such important allies as Japan, Australia, South Korea, Taiwan, and Europe, and cast doubt on American claims to represent "rules-based" international order and fairness. In contrast, Japan has remained far more supportive of trade agreements and played a major role in promoting TPP-11 and the Regional Comprehensive Economic Partnership (RCEP), an economically modest but politically significant grouping that includes China but not the United States or India. Coordinating trade and industrial policies with the United States and continuing to exert leadership in regional and global trade negotiations in the absence of American support are likely to pose ongoing challenges for Japanese policymakers.

Balancing Energy Sources and Carriers

A final fundamental challenge is improving and balancing competing energy sources. In the short run, Japan has little choice but to continue relying heavily on fossil fuels. Recent energy documents have expressed a more positive attitude toward renewables, particularly offshore wind, which is less constrained by difficulties acquiring appropriate sites, but the hopes and passions of policymakers are still tied to nuclear power. The marginal cost of electricity from newly reopened or newly re-licensed nuclear plants will be low, but many plants will be too expensive to restart. Renewables will continue to be plagued by intermittency, low density, and limited grid capacity. Key questions are how quickly developers can cut the cost of offshore wind and reduce the cost of energy storage, and how quickly next-generation nuclear power plants can obtain licenses and come online. If the history of the nuclear power industry is any guide, development and licensing are likely to take longer than expected. If the delay is too great, nuclear power plants could be undercut by the ever-decreasing cost of renewables and storage, even in Japan, and become expensive stranded assets. It is also possible, however, that nuclear power could play a modest role as a clean and relatively economical source of hydrogen.

Similarly, regional utilities would like to use hydrogen and ammonia to extend the life of their existing fossil fuel plants, but they may well struggle to cut costs and improve environmental quality. Technological progress has been significant but the challenges remain formidable. Policymakers will have to decide how many resources to pour into hydrogen and ammonia.

The Future of Industrial Policy in Japan and Its Northeast Asian Neighbors

Japan is not alone in witnessing a revival of industrial policy. Deteriorating economic performance, expanding security threats, and the increasing shakiness of the international trade and investment regime impinge at least as tightly on South Korea, Taiwan, and China. The drift from economic openness of the United States, the European Union, and the United Kingdom casts a shadow across all of northeast Asia. As in Japan, policymakers in South Korea and Taiwan are hard-pressed to point to unambiguous examples of successful industrial policy.

China seems more successful, particularly in green technology, but it has paid a high price for its successes in the form of massive subsidies, has still not completely caught up with world technology leaders, and has unique structural problems, including the inefficiency of state-owned enterprises and the financial fragility of the bloated property sector. All four countries face serious macro-economic difficulties and demographic pressures that are beyond the reach of industrial policy, including sagging domestic demand, slumping growth in total factor productivity, fraught gender relations, and plummeting birth rates.

The growing appeal of industrial policy over the last decade and more is easy to understand. Economic theory and empirical examples, not least from China, show that industrial policy can be effective, with important applications for national economic security. But it can also fail or come at a high price in budgetary outlays and reduced economic efficiency. It may also be subject to a fallacy of composition: if many countries seek to protect and promote the same sectors at the same time, they may offset each other and undermine overall efficiency. Given the economic and military threats facing Japan and its Northeast Asian neighbors, industrial policy is unlikely to disappear completely, but as its costs and frustrations become more apparent, its relative importance may shrink again.

References

Åhman, Max. 2006. "Government Policy and the Development of Electric Vehicles in Japan." *Energy Policy* 34 (4):433–443.

AIST. 2020. "Employees and Budget." National Institute of Advanced Industrial Science and Technology, accessed July 20, 2022. www.aist.go.jp/aist_e/about_aist/facts_figures/fact_figures.html.

Amakudari-log. "Amakudari-log," accessed July 2, 2022. https://amakudari-log.site/workers.

Amsden, Alice H. 1989. *Asia's Next Giant: South Korea and Late Industrialization*. New York: Oxford University Press.

Amsden, Alice H., and Wan-wen Chu. 2003. *Beyond Late Development: Taiwan's Upgrading Policies*. Cambridge, MA: MIT Press.

Arias, Jonathan. 2019. *Hydrogen and Fuel Cells in Japan*. Tokyo: EU-Japan Centre for Industrial Cooperation.

Atchison, Julian. 2022. "JERA Targets 50% Ammonia-Coal Co-firing by 2030." *Ammoniaenergy*, January 21, 2022. https://www.ammoniaenergy.org/articles/jera-targets-50-ammonia-coal-co-firing-by-2030/.

Bateman, Jon. 2022. *US-China Technological "Decoupling": A Strategy and Policy Framework*. Washington, DC: Carnegie Endowment for International Peace.

Beason, Richard, and David E. Weinstein. 1996. "Growth, Economies of Scale, and Targeting in Japan (1955–1990)." *Review of Economics & Statistics* 78 (2):286.

Behling, Noriko, Mark C. Williams, and Shunsuke Managi. 2016. "Japan Has Great Expectations for a Hydrogen Society." *ECS Transactions* 71 (1):1–12.

Behling, Noriko Hikosaka. 2013. *Fuel Cells: Current Technology Challenges and Future Research Needs*. Amsterdam: Elsevier.

Benson, Emily, and Catharine Mouradian. 2023. *How Do the United States and Its Partners Approach Economic Security?* Washington, DC: The Center for Strategic and International Studies (CSIS).

BlackRock. 2024. "Time to Shine: A Compelling Case for Japanese Equities." www.blackrock.com/hk/en/insights/japanese-equities-market-compelling#.

BloombergNEF. 2022. *Japan's Costly Ammonia Coal Co-firing Strategy*. New York: BloombergNEF.

Bonvillian, William Boone, Richard Van Atta, and Patrick Windham. 2019. *The DARPA Model for Transformative Technologies: Perspectives on the US Defense Advanced Research Projects Agency*. Cambridge: Open Book.

Bossler, Annette. 2012. *Wind Power in Japan – An Overview.* Bremen, ME: Main(e) International Consulting.

Boyd, Richard. 1986. "Government-Industry Relations in Japan: Access, Communication and Competitive Collaboration." In *Comparative Government — Industry Relations: Western Europe, United States, and Japan*, edited by Stephen Wilks, and Maurice Wright, 61–90. Oxford: Oxford University Press.

Cabinet Secretariat. 2022a. "経済施策を一体的に講ずることによる安全保障の確保の推進に関する法律案 (An Act on the Promotion of Security Assurance through the Integrated Implementation of Economic Measures)," accessed June 24, 2022. www.cas.go.jp/jp/houan/208.html.

Cabinet Secretariat. 2022b. "資料4—ご説明資料 (Document 4: Explanatory Materials)." 内閣官房経済安全保障法制準備室 (Economic Security Legislation Preparatory Office, Cabinet Secretariat), Last Modified July 25, 2022. www.cas.go.jp/jp/seisaku/keizai_anzen_hosyohousei/4index.html.

Cabinet Secretariat GX Implementation Committee. 2022. GX実現に向けた基本方針 ~今後10年を見据えたロードマップ (*Draft Basic Policy for Realization of GX [Green Transformation]: Roadmap for the Next 10 Years*). Tokyo: 内閣官房 GX Implementation Committee. https://www.cas.go.jp/jp/seisaku/gx_jikkou_kaigi/pdf/kihon.pdf.

Cabinet Secretariat Personnel Division. 2022. "女性国家公務員の採用状況のフォローアップ(Follow-Up Results of the Recruitment of Female National Public Servants)." June 1. https://www.cas.go.jp/jp/gaiyou/jimu/jinjikyoku/files/20220601_followup.pdf.

Calder, Kent E. 1993. *Strategic Capitalism: Private Business and Public Purpose in Japanese Industrial Finance.* Princeton, NJ: Princeton University Press.

Callon, Scott. 1995. *Divided Sun: MITI and the Breakdown of Japanese High-Tech Industrial Policy, 1975–1993.* Stanford: Stanford University Press.

Chiavacci, David, and Carola Hommerich, eds. 2017. *Social Inequality in Post-Growth Japan: Transformation during Economic and Demographic Stagnation.* London: Routledge.

Choi, Jaedo, and Andrei A. Levchenko. 2021. *The Long-Term Effects of Industrial Policy.* Washington, DC: National Bureau of Economic Research.

Daigle, Brian, and Samantha DeCarlo. 2021. *Rare Earths and the US Electronics Sector: Supply Chain Developments and Trends.* Washington, DC: Office of Industries, US International Trade Commission.

Doner, Richard F., Gregory W. Noble, and John Ravenhill. 2021. *The Political Economy of Automotive Industrialization in East Asia.* Oxford: Oxford University Press.

Downie, Christian, and Llewelyn Hughes. 2020. "Will Japan Continue to Finance International Coal Projects?" *East Asian Forum*. https://eastasia forum.org/2020/08/18/will-japan-continue-to-finance-international-coal-pro jects/.

Elder, Mark. 2003. "METI and Industrial Policy in Japan: Change and Continuity." In *Japan's Managed Globalization: Adapting to the Twenty-First Century*, edited by Ulrike Schaede and William Grimes, 159–190. Armonk, NY: M.E. Sharpe.

Evenett, Simon, and Johannes Fritz. 2023. "Revisiting the China – Japan Rare Earths Dispute of 2010." *VoxEU*, July 19. https://cepr.org/voxeu/columns/ revisiting-china-japan-rare-earths-dispute-2010.

FBI. 2019. "China: The Risk to Corporate America." Federal Bureau of Investigation, accessed June 28, 2022. www.fbi.gov/file-repository/china-risk-to-corporate-america-2019.pdf.

Feigenbaum, Evan A. 2003. *China's Techno-Warriors: National Security and Strategic Competition from the Nuclear to the Information Age*. Stanford: Stanford University Press.

Ferry, Tim. 2020. "Offshore Wind Industry Struggles with Localisation." *Euroview*, November 24, 2020. https://euroview.ecct.com.tw/category-inside.php?id=412.

Friedman, David, and Richard J. Samuels. 1993. "How to Succeed without Really Flying: The Japanese Aircraft Industry and Japan's Technology Ideology." In *Regionalism and Rivalry: Japan and the United States in Pacific Asia*, edited by Jeffrey A. Frankel, and Miles Kahler, 251–320. Chicago, IL: University of Chicago Press.

Fujimoto, Takahiro. 2004. 日本のもの造り哲学 *[Japan's Philosophy of the Art of Making Things]*. 東京: 日本経済新聞社. Tokyo: Nihon Keizai Shinbunsha.

Fuller, Douglas B. 2019. "Growth, Upgrading and Limited Catch-Up in China's Semiconductor Industry." In *Policy, Regulation and Innovation in China's Electricity and Telecom Industries*, edited by Loren Brandt, and Thomas G. Rawski, 262–303. Cambridge: Cambridge University Press.

Fuller, Douglas B. 2021. "China's Counter-Strategy to American Export Controls in Integrated Circuits." *China Leadership Monitor* (67, Spring). https://www.prcleader.org/post/china-s-counter-strategy-to-american-export-controls-in-integrated-circuits.

Fuller, Douglas B. 2022. "The Increasing Irrelevance of Industrial Policy in Taiwan, 2016–2020." In *Taiwan during the First Administration of Tsai Ing-wen*, edited by Gunter Schubert, and Chun-Yi Lee, 128–141. New York: Routledge.

Goto, Mika, and Toshiyuki Sueyoshi. 2016. "Electricity Market Reform in Japan after Fukushima." *Economics of Energy & Environmental Policy* 5 (1):15–30.

Graham, Euan. 2005. *Japan's Sea Lane Security, 1940–2004: A Matter of Life and Death?* Oxford: Routledge.

Grey, Eva. 2017. "Is Japan's Bullet Train an Affordable Export?" *Railway Technology*, January 24, 2017. https://www.railway-technology.com/features/featureis-japans-bullet-train-an-affordable-export-5723022/.

Guo, Eileen, Jess Aloe, and Karen Hao. 2021. "The US Crackdown on Chinese Economic Espionage Is a Mess: We Have the Data to Show It." *MIT Technology Review*, December 2, 2021. https://www.technologyreview.com/2021/12/02/1040656/china-initative-us-justice-department/.

Hannas, William C., James Mulvenon, and Anna B. Puglisi. 2013. *Chinese Industrial Espionage: Technology Acquisition and Military Modernisation*. London: Routledge.

Henderson, David R. 1983. "The Myth of MITI: Individual Initiative, Not Central Planning, Is the Main Source of Japan's Growth." *Fortune* August 8, 1983:113–116.

Hill, Stephen, Aileen Ionescu-Somers, Alicia Coduras, et al. 2022. *Global Entrepreneurship Monitor 2021/2022 Global Report*. London: Global Entrepreneurship Research Association.

Holroyd, Carin. 2018. *Green Japan: Environmental Technologies, Innovation Policy, and the Pursuit of Green Growth*. Toronto: University of Toronto Press.

Hood, Christopher P. 2007. "Bullets and Trains: Exporting Japan's Shinkansen to China and Taiwan." *Japan Focus* 5 (3), Article ID 2367.

Hoshi, Takeo, and Phillip Y. Lipscy. 2021. "The Political Economy of the Abe Government." In *The Political Economy of the Abe Government and Abenomics Reforms*, edited by Takeo Hoshi, and Phillip Y. Lipscy, 3–39. Cambridge: Cambridge University Press.

Hourihan, Matt, and Alessandra Zimmermann. 2022. "U.S. R&D and Innovation in a Global Context: 2022 Data Update." American Association for the Advancement of Science (AAAS), Last Modified May 10. www.aaas.org/sites/default/files/2022-05/AAAS%20Global%20R%26D%20Update%20May%202022.pdf.

Hymans, Jacques E. C. 2021. "Losing Steam: Why Does Japan Produce So Little Geothermal Power?" *Social Science Japan Journal* 24 (1):45–65.

IEA. 2022. Average Power Generation Construction Time (Capacity Weighted), 2010–2018. Paris: International Energy Agency.

INCJ. 2018. INCJ to Sell Part of Its Shares in Renesas Electronics Corporation. Innovation Network Corporation of Japan.

Intarakumnerd, Patarapong. 2011. "Two Models of Research Technology Organisations in Asia." *Science, Technology, and Society* 16 (1):11–28.

IRENA. 2015. *Renewable Energy Capacity Statistics*. Abu Dhabi: International Renewable Energy Agency.

IRENA. 2021. *Renewable Energy Auctions in Japan: Context, Design and Results*. Abu Dhabi: International Renewable Energy Agency.

IRENA. 2022a. Energy Profile: Japan. Abu Dhabi: International Renewable Energy Agency.

IRENA. 2022b. *Geopolitics of the Energy Transformation: The Hydrogen Factor*. Abu Dhabi: International Renewable Energy Agency.

IRENA. 2022c. Renewable Energy Statistics 2022. Abu Dhabi: International Renewable Energy Agency.

IRENA. 2022d. *Renewable Power Generation Costs in 2021*. Abu Dhabi: International Rnewable Energy Agency.

Ishitani, Hisashi, and Yasuko Baba. 2008. "The Japanese Strategy on R&D for Fuel-Cell Technology and On-Road Test Verification of Fuel-Cell Vehicles." In *Making Choices about Hydrogen: Transport Issues for Developing Countries*, edited by Lynn K. Mytelka, and Grant Boyle, 39–63. Ottawa: International Development Research Centre.

JANE. "Policy Theme List." Japan Association of New Economy, accessed September 2, 2022. https://jane.or.jp/en/policy/.

JAPIA. "Japan Auto Parts Industries Association." Accessed September 2, 2024. www.japia.or.jp/en/top/.

JCI. 2022. "Now Is the Time to Accelerate Renewable Energy Deployment– Calling for Stronger Climate Change Action in the Midst of the Fossil Energy Crisis–." Last Modified June 17, 2022. https://japanclimate.org/english/news-topics/jci-message-re-release/.

JEPIC. 2022. *The Electric Power Industry in Japan 2022*. Tokyo: The Japan Electric Power Information Center (JEPIC).

JETRO. "Japan's International Trade in Goods (Yearly)." Japan External Trade Organization, accessed June 24, 2022. www.jetro.go.jp/en/reports/statistics.html.

Jiang, Yifan, Baiyu Gao, and Sam Geall. 2022. "China's Five Year Plan for Energy: One Eye on Security Today, One on a Low-Carbon Future." *China Dialogue*, June 23, 2022. https://dialogue.earth/en/energy/chinas-five-year-plan-for-energy-one-eye-on-security-today-one-on-a-low-carbon-future/.

JISF. 2021. "Basic Policy of the Japan Steel Industry on 2050 Carbon Neutrality Aimed by the Japanese Government." Japan Iron and Steel Federation, Last

Modified February 15, 2021, accessed September 24, 2022. www.jisf.or.jp/en/activity/climate/documents/CN2050_eng_201210215.pdf.

Johnson, Chalmers. 1982. *MITI and the Japanese Miracle: The Growth of Industrial Policy, 1925–1975*. Stanford: Stanford University Press.

Juhász, Réka, Nathan J. Lane, and Dani Rodrik. 2023. The New Economics of Industrial Policy. National Bureau of Economic Research. Working Paper 31538.

Kamakura, Natsuki. 2022. "From Globalising to Regionalising to Reshoring Value Chains? The Case of Japan's Semiconductor Industry." *Cambridge Journal of Regions, Economy and Society* 15 (2):261–277. https://doi.org/10.1093/cjres/rsac010.

Kamba, Katsuhiro. 2015. "審議会人事に関する一考察──財政制度等審議会と産業構造審議会を例として── (An Investigation into Shingikai Personnel: Case Studies of the Fiscal System Council and the Industrial Structure Council)." 八戸学院大学紀要 *(Proceedings of the Hachinoe Graduate School)* 50:1–9.

Kamikawa, Ryūnoshin. 2024. "Promotion or Regulation? Blurred Lines in Japan's Nuclear Energy Policy." www.nippon.com/en/in-depth/d00952/.

Kang, Nahee, and Kahee Jo. 2021. "State – Business Relations in Flux: Capturing the Structural Power of Business in South Korea's Green Industrial Policy." *Journal of Contemporary Asia* 51 (5):713–736. https://doi.org/10.1080/00472336.2021.1915362.

Kaplan, Eugene J. 1972. *Japan: The Government-Business Relationship – A Guide for the American Businessman*. Washington, DC: U.S. Bureau of International Commerce.

Katada, Saori N. 2020. *Japan's New Regional Reality: Geoeconomic Strategy in the Asia-Pacific*. New York: Columbia University Press.

Katz, Richard. 2022. "Korea Has Already Passed Japan in Per Capita GDP." *The Oriental Economist* (March 9).

Katz, Richard. 2023. *The Contest for Japan's Economic Future: Entrepreneurs vs. Corporate Giants*. New York: Oxford University Press.

Kawashima, Nobuko. 2018. "'Cool Japan' and Creative Industries: An Evaluation of Economic Policies for Popular Culture Industries in Japan." In *Asian Cultural Flows: Cultural Policies, Creative Industries, and Media Consumers*, edited by Nobuko Kawashima, and Hye-Kyung Lee, 19–36. Singapore: Springer.

Keidanren. "経団連について　役員名簿 (About Keidanren: List of Directors)," accessed August 29, 2022. www.keidanren.or.jp/profile/yakuin/pro003.html.

Kelly, Tim, Cyril Altmeyer, and Colin Packham. 2016. "How France Sank Japan's $40 Billion Australian Submarine Dream." *Reuters*, April 29, 2016.

www.reuters.com/article/us-australia-submarines-japan-defence-in-idUSKCN0XQ1FC.

Kennedy, Scott. 2005. *The Business of Lobbying in China.* Cambridge, MA: Harvard University Press.

Kikkawa, Takeo. 2004. 日本電力業発展のダイナミズム *(Dynamism of Development in the Japanese Electric Power Industry).* Nagoya: Nagoya University Press.

Kim, Sung-Young, and Elizabeth Thurbon. 2015. "Developmental Environmentalism: Explaining South Korea's Ambitious Pursuit of Green Growth." *Politics & Society* 43 (2):213–240.

Kioxia. 2024. "Kioxia and Western Digital's Joint Venture to Receive up to 150 Billion Yen Government Subsidy for Yokkaichi and Kitakami Plants." Last Modified February 6. https://apac.kioxia.com/en-apac/about/news/2024/20240206-1.html.

Kitamura, Shigeru, and Tsuyoshi Oyabu. 2022. 経済安全保障: 異形の大国、中国を直視せよ *Keizai anzen hoshō: igyō no taikoku chūgoku o chokushi seyo.* Tokyo: 中央公論新社 Chūōkōronshinsha.

Koh, Byung Chul. 1989. *Japan's Administrative Elite.* Berkeley: University of California Press.

Koppenborg, Florentine. 2023. *Japan's Nuclear Disaster and the Politics of Safety Governance.* Ithaca, NY: Cornell University Press.

Koumuin-senmon.com. "【2025年】公務員試験の難易度を格付ランキング (Ranking [Governmental Bodies by] the Difficulty of the Civil Service Examination, 2025)," accessed January 3, 2025. https://koumuin-senmon.com/entry99.html?msclkid=2f18408bce8a11ec94dae54d89adee53#i2.

Krugman, Paul R. 1994. "Competitiveness: A Dangerous Obsession." *Foreign Affairs* 73 (2):28–44.

Kushida, Kenji E., and Phillip Y. Lipscy, eds. 2013. *Japan under the DPJ: The Politics of Transition and Governance.* Stanford: Asia-Pacific Research Center.

Lardy, Nicholas R. 2019. *The State Strikes Back: The End of Economic Reform in China?* Washington, D.C.: Peterson Institute for International Economics.

Lazard. 2021. Lazard's Levelized Cost of Energy Analysis – Version 15.0. New York: Lazard. https://www.lazard.com/media/sptlfats/lazards-levelized-cost-of-energy-version-150-vf.pdf.

Lee, Yeonho, and Hak-Ryul Kim. 2018. "Economic Crises and Augmenting Financial Bureaucratic Power in South Korea." *The Pacific Review* 31 (3):352–372.

Leng, Zhihui, Han Sun, Jinhua Cheng, Hai Wang, and Zhen Yao. 2021. "China's Rare Earth Industry Technological Innovation Structure and Driving Factors: A Social Network Analysis Based on Patents." *Resources Policy* 73:102233.

Maclachlan, Patricia L., and Kay Shimizu. 2021. "The Farm Lobby and Agricultural Policy in Japan." In *The Oxford Handbook of Japanese Politics*, edited by Robert J. Pekkanen, and Saadia M. Pekkanen, 415–431. New York: Oxford University Press.

Matsuo, Yuhji, and Hisanori Nei. 2019. "An Analysis of the Historical Trends in Nuclear Power Plant Construction Costs: The Japanese Experience." *Energy Policy* 124:180–198. https://doi.org/10.1016/j.enpol.2018.08.067.

McGregor, Richard. 2021. "Bombard the Headquarters: Xi Jinping's Crackdown Keeps Growing." *Nikkei Asia*, September 29. https://asia.nik kei.com/Spotlight/The-Big-Story/Bombard-the-headquarters-Xi-Jinping-s-crackdown-keeps-growing.

Mercado, Stephen C. 1995. "The YS-11 Project and Japan's Aerospace Potential." *JPRI Occasional Paper* (5). https://jpri.org/document/the-ys-11-project-and-japans-aerospace-potential/.

METI. 2010. 産業構造ビジョン 2010 (Industrial Structure Vision 2010). http://www.japic.org/pdf_sys%20/20100624_04.pdf.

METI. 2017. "New Industrial Structure Vision." www.meti.go.jp/english/publi cations/pdf/vision_171222.pdf.

METI. 2020. 産業技術ビジョン 2020 (Industrial Technology Vision 2020: The New and Old Issue is Calling our Transformation [sic]). https://www8 .cao.go.jp/cstp/tyousakai/kihon6/5kai/sanko5.pdf.

METI. 2021a. エネルギー基本計画 (6th Strategic Energy Plan). Tokyo: METI.

METI. 2021b. グリーンイノベーション基金事業 の基本方針 (Basic Policy for Green Innovation Fund Projects). Tokyo: METI.

METI. 2021c. "梶山経済産業大臣の閣議後記者会見の概要 (Summary of Post-Cabinet Meeting Press Conference by METI Minister Kajiyama)." June 18, 2021.

METI. 2022a. "Battery Industry Strategy – Interim Summary." Ministry of Economy, Trade and Industry, Last Modified April 22, 2022. www.meti.go .jp/english/report/pdf/0520_001a.pdf.

METI. 2022b. 令和3年度エネルギーに関する年次報告 (エネルギー白書 2022) (Annual Report on Energy, Fiscal Year 2021 [White Paper on Energy 2022]).

METI. 2022c. "経済産業省関係令和4年度補正予算案のポイント (Key Points of the Proposed FY2022 Supplemental Budget Related to METI)."

Accessed December 23, 2024. www.meti.go.jp/main/yosan/yosan_fy2022/hosei/pdf/hosei2_yosan_point.pdf.

METI, and MLITT. 2024. 「モビリティDX戦略 (案)」<概要版> (Mobility DX Strategy (Draft) <Outline>).

METI ANRE. 2022. 令和2年度(2020年度)における エネルギー需給実績 (確報) (Actual Energy Demand and Supply in FY2020 (Confirmed Data)). Tokyo: METI Agency for Natural Resources and Energy.

Ministry of Finance. "Budget," accessed December 23, 2024. www.mof.go.jp/english/policy/budget/budget/index.html.

Ministry of Finance Budget Bureau. 2022. 令和4年度特別会計予算 (2022 Special Accounts Budget).

Ministry of Finance Budget Bureau. "Various Years." 一般会計予算 (General Account Budget)." https://www.mof.go.jp/policy/budget/budger_workflow/index.html.

Misawa, Kazufumi. 2005. *Naze nihonsha wa sekai saikyō na no ka [Why Are Japanese Cars the Strongest in the World?]*. Tokyo: PHP Kenkyūjo.

Miura, Mari. 2012. *Welfare through Work: Conservative Ideas, Partisan Dynamics, and Social Protection in Japan*. Ithaca, NY: Cornell University Press.

Mizuno, Emi. 2014. "Overview of Wind Energy Policy and Development in Japan." *Renewable and Sustainable Energy Reviews* 40:999–1018.

Mori, Kazuo. 2014. "How Corporate Japan Lost Its 'Voice': The Plight of Keidanren in the Post–Japan Inc. Era." March 10. www.nippon.com/ja/currents/d00111/.

Munoz, Juan Felipe. 2022. "The Hydrogen Powered Car Is Alive: Sales Up by 84 Percent in 2021." Last Modified March 17, 2022. www.motor1.com/news/574229/hydrogen-powered-car-alive-sales-up-84-percent/.

Murakami, Tomoko, and Venkatachalam Anbumozhi. 2021. Global Situation of Small Modular Reactor Development and Deployment. Jakarta: Economic Research Institute for ASEAN and East Asia (ERIA).

Mutoh, Hiromichi. 1988. "The Automobile Industry." In *Industrial Policy of Japan*, edited by Ryutaro Komiya, Masahiro Okuno, and Kotaro Suzumura, 37–331. San Diego, CA: Academic Press.

Nakano, Masashi. 2009. 天下りの研究: その実態とメカニズムの解明. (A Study of Amakudari: Elucidating the Realities and Mechanisms of Amakudari). Tokyo: Akashi Books.

National Personnel Authority. 2021. "2021年度国家公務員採用総合職試験 の合格者発表 (Announcement of Successful Candidates for the 2021 National Civil Service Recruitment Comprehensive Examination)." Last Modified June 21. www.jinji.go.jp/kisya/2106/2021sougousaigou.html.

Naughton, Barry. 2018. *The Chinese Economy: Adaptation and Growth*. 2nd ed. Cambridge, MA: MIT Press.

Naughton, Barry. 2021. *The Rise of China's Industrial Policy, 1978 to 2020*. Mexico City: Universidad Nacional Autónomica de México, Facultad de Economía México.

NEDO. "Background Information." New Energy and Industrial Technology Development Organization, accessed June 21, 2022. www.nedo.go.jp/english/introducing/introducing_profile.html.

NEDO. 2022. グリーンイノベーション基金事業「燃料アンモニアのサプライチェーン構築」に着手 (Launching the Green Innovation Fund Project "Establishment of Fuel Ammonia Supply Chain"). Tokyo: New Energy and Industrial Technology Development Organization.

Noble, Gregory W. 1992. *Flying Apart? Japanese-American Negotiations over the FSX Fighter Plane*. Berkeley: University of California Institute of International Studies.

Noble, Gregory W. 1998. *Collective Action in East Asia: How Ruling Parties Shape Industrial Policy, Cornell Studies in Political Economy*. Ithaca, NY: Cornell University Press.

Noble, Gregory W. 2002. "Reform and Continuity in Japan's *Shingikai* Deliberation Councils." In *Japanese Governance: Beyond Japan Inc.*, edited by Jennifer Amyx, and Peter Drysdale, 113–133. London: Routledge Curzon.

Noble, Gregory W. 2016. "Toward a Responsive Two-Party System? A Review of 'Series: Japanese Politics'." *Social Science Japan Journal* 19 (1):85–97. https://doi.org/10.1093/ssjj/jyw014.

Noble, Gregory W. 2017. "Government-Business Relations in Democratizing Asia." In *Routledge Handbook of Democratization in East Asia*, edited by Tun-jen Cheng, and Yun-han Chu, 427–442. New York: Routledge.

Noble, Gregory W. 2019. "Staffing the State with Women." In *Beyond the Gender Gap in Japan*, edited by Gill Steel, 229–246. Ann Arbor: University of Michigan Press.

Noble, Gregory W. 2021. "METI's Miraculous Comeback and the Uncertain Future of Japanese Industrial Policy." In *The Oxford Handbook of Japanese Politics*, edited by Robert J. Pekkanen, and Saadia M. Pekkanen. New York: Oxford University Press.

Nuclear Sub-Committee. 2022. 今後の原子力政策の方向性と実現に向けたアクションプラン(案) (Future Direction of Nuclear Energy Policy and Action Plan for Its Realization (Draft)). Tokyo: 経済産業省　第34回 総合資源エネルギー調査会 電力・ガス事業分科会 原子力小委員会.

Odaka, Konosuke, ed. 2013. 通商産業政策史 *1980–2000* 第一巻 総論 *[History of Japan's Trade and Industry Policy 1980–2000 (Volume 1): General Overview]*. Tokyo: Tsūshō Sangyō Seisakushi Hensan Iinkai.

OECD. "Average Annual Wages," accessed June 17, 2022. https://stats.oecd.org/Index.aspx?DataSetCode=AV_AN_WAGE.

OECD. "Gross Domestic Spending on R&D, Total, % of GDP, 2000 – 2020." Organisation for Economic Co-operation and Development, Main Science and Technology Indicators, accessed July 2, 2022. https://data.oecd.org/rd/gross-domestic-spending-on-r-d.htm.

OECD. 2001. *Competition in Electricity Markets*. Paris: Organisation for Economic Cooperation and Development.

Ohta, Hiroshi, and Brendan Barrett. 2023. "Politics of Climate Change and Energy Policy in Japan: Is Green Transformation Likely?" *Earth System Governance* 17:100187.

Okuno-Fujiwara, Masahiro. 1988. "Interdependence of Industries, Coordination Failure and Strategic Promotion of an Industry." *Journal of International Economics* 25:25–43.

Openwork. "総合評価ランキング (Overall Evaluation Ranking)," accessed July 22, 2022. www.vorkers.com/company_list?field=&pref=&src_str=&sort=2.

Otmazgin, Nissim. 2020. "State Intervention Does Not Support the Development of the Media Sector: Lessons from Korea and Japan." *Global Policy* 11 (S2):40–46. https://doi.org/10.1111/1758-5899.12821.

Ozaki, Toshiya. 2012. "Open Trade, Closed Industry: The Japanese Aerospace Industry in the Evolution of Economic Nationalism and Implications for Globalization." In *Globalization and Economic Nationalism in Asia*, edited by Anthony P. D'Acosta, 135–156. Oxford: Oxford University Press.

Ozawa, Kōji. 2019. "キャリア官僚"合格者倍増する意外な私大 なぜ東大生が激減しているのか (Surprising Private Universities Double the Number of Exam-Passing 'Career Bureaucrats' – Why Is the Number of Tokyo University Students Dramatically Decreasing?)." *President*, January 18.

Park, Gene. 2011. *Spending Without Taxation FILP: and the Politics of Public Finance in Japan*. Stanford, CA: Stanford University Press.

Pearson, Margaret, Meg Rithmire, and Kellee Tsai. 2023. *The State and Capitalism in China*. Cambridge: Cambridge University Press.

Pekkanen, Robert J., Benjamin Nyblade, and Ellis S. Krauss. 2014. "The Logic of Ministerial Selection: Electoral System and Cabinet Appointments in Japan." *Social Science Japan Journal* 17 (1):3–22.

Pekkanen, Robert J., Steven R. Reed, and Ethan Scheiner. 2016. "Conclusion: Japan's Bait-and-Switch Election 2014." In *Japan Decides 2014: The*

Japanese General Election, edited by Robert J. Pekkanen, Steven R. Reed, and Ethan Scheiner, 265–278. Basingstoke: Palgrave Macmillan.

Pekkanen, Saadia M. 2003. *Picking Winners? From Technology Catch-Up to the Space Race in Japan*. Stanford, CA: Stanford University Press.

Pekkanen, Saadia M. 2005. "Bilateralism, Multilateralism, or Regionalism? Japan's Trade Forum Choices." *Journal of East Asian Studies* 5 (1):77–103.

Public-Private Council on Enhancement of Industrial Competitiveness for Offshore Wind Power Generation. 2020. Vision for Offshore Wind Power Industry (1st). Tokyo: METI.

REI. 2022a. 日本の水素戦略の再検討 「水素社会」の幻想を超えて (Reexamining Japan's Hydrogen Strategy: Transcending the Illusion of a "Hydrogen Society"). Tokyo: 自然エネルギー財団.

REI. 2022b. 欧州のエネルギー危機、自然エネルギーが電気料金の軽減に (Europe's Energy Crisis – Renewable Energy to Reduce Electricity Prices). Tokyo: 自然エネルギー財団.

REI. 2023. "Solar PV." Renewable Energy Institute, accessed January 1, 2023. www.renewable-ei.org/en/statistics/re/.

REN21. 2022. *Renewables 2022 Global Status Report*. Paris: REN21 (Renewable Energy Policy Network for the 21st Century).

Samuels, Richard J. 1987. *The Business of the Japanese State: Energy Markets in Comparative and Historical Perspective*. Ithaca, NY: Cornell University Press.

Samuels, Richard J. 1994. *"Rich Nation, Strong Army": National Security and the Technological Transformation of Japan*. Ithaca, NY: Cornell University Press.

Sasaki, Kenshō. 2016. 財界支配—日本経団連の実相 *(Business Community Domination – The Reality of Nippon Keidanren)*. Tokyo: Shinnihon.

Schaede, Ulrike. 2020. *The Business Reinvention of Japan: How to Make Sense of the New Japan and Why It Matters*. Stanford: Stanford Business Books.

Schaede, Ulrike, and Kay Shimizu. 2022. *The Digital Transformation and Japan's Political Economy*. Cambridge: Cambridge University Press.

Schwartz, Frank J. 1998. *Advice and Consent: The Politics of Consultation in Japan*. Cambridge: Cambridge University Press.

Sheftalovich, Zoya. 2021. "Why Australia Wanted Out of Its French Submarine Deal." *Politico*, September 16, 2021.

Shimizu, Masato. 2016. "Ikioizuku 'Abe-keisanshō naikaku' no iki-saki (Wither the 'Abe-METI Cabinet' as it gains momentum)." *Nihon Keizai Shinbun*, June 21. www.nikkei.com/article/DGXMZO03816140Q6 A620C1000000/.

SIPRI. "The SIPRI Military Expenditure Database." Stockholm International Peace Research Institute, accessed June 23, 2022. https://milex.sipri.org/sipri.

State Council. 2015. "国务院关于印发《中国制造 2025》的通知 (Announcement of the State Council's Publication of 'Made in China 2025')," accessed July 2, 2022. www.gov.cn/zhengce/content/2015-05/19/content_9784.htm.

Statistics Bureau of Japan. "Table 18–1 Yearly Average of Monthly Disbursements per Household (Two-or-More-Person Households)," accessed June 17, 2022. www.stat.go.jp/data/kakei/longtime/zuhyou/18-01-an.xls.

Suehiro, Akira. 2008. *Catch-Up Industrialization: The Trajectory and Prospects of East Asian Economics*. Translated by Tom Gill. Singapore: NUS Press.

Takenaka, Harukata. 2021. "Expansion of the Japanese Prime Minister's Power and Transformation of Japanese Politics." In *The Political Economy of the Abe Government and Abenomics Reforms*, edited by Takeo Hoshi, and Phillip Y. Lipscy, 43–67. Cambridge: Cambridge University Press.

The White House. 2021. Building Resilient Supply Chains, Revitalizing American Manufacturing, and Fostering Broad-Based Growth: 100-Day Reviews under Executive Order 14017. Washington, DC: The White House.

Thorbecke, Willem. 2019. "Why Japan Lost Its Comparative Advantage in Producing Electronic Parts and Components." *Journal of the Japanese and International Economies* 54:101050. https://doi.org/10.1016/j.jjie.2019.101050.

Tilton, Mark. 1996. *Restrained Trade: Cartels in Japan's Basic Materials Industries*. Ithaca, NY: Cornell University Press.

Tomain, Joseph P. 2002. "The Past and Future of Electricity Regulation." *Environmental Law* 32:435–474.

Tung, An-Chi. 2001. "Taiwan's Semiconductor Industry: What the State Did and Did Not." *Review of Development Economics* 5 (2):266–288.

Uno, Hideki. 2022. Japanese Semiconductor Industrial Policymaking in the Twenty-First Century. Washington, DC: CSIS.

Vogel, Steven K. 1996. *Freer Markets, More Rules: Regulatory Reform in Advanced Industrial Countries*. Ithaca, NY: Cornell University Press.

Vogel, Steven K. 2021. "The Rise and Fall of the Japanese Bureaucracy." In *The Oxford Handbook of Japanese Politics*, edited by Robert J. Pekkanen, and Saadia M. Pekkanen, 101–116. New York: Oxford University Press.

Wade, Robert. 1990. *Governing the Market: Economic Theory and the Role of Government in East Asian Industrialization*. Princeton, NJ: Princeton University Press.

WHO. 2021. New WHO Global Air Quality Guidelines Aim to Save Millions of Lives from Air Pollution. Geneva: World Health Organization.

Wong, Joseph. 2011. *Betting on Biotech: Innovation and the Limits of Asia's Developmental State.* Ithaca, NY: Cornell University Press.

World Bank. "GDP (current US$) – China," accessed June 17, 2022. https://data .worldbank.org/indicator/NY.GDP.MKTP.CD?locations=CN&name_ desc=false.

World Bank. "Net Primary Income (BoP, current US$) – Japan," accessed September 2, 2024. https://data.worldbank.org/indicator/BN.GSR.FCTY .CD?locations=JP.

World Bank. "Net Trade in Goods and Services (BoP, current US$) – Japan," accessed September 2, 2024. https://data.worldbank.org/indicator/BN.GSR .GNFS.CD?locations=JP.

World Bank. 2020. Global Photovoltaic Power Potential by Country. Washington DC: World Bank.

Wray, Christopher. 2020. "Hudson Institute, Video Event: China's Attempt to Influence U.S. Institutions, the Threat Posed by the Chinese Government and the Chinese Communist Party to the Economic and National Security of the United States." FBI. www.fbi.gov/news/speeches/the-threat-posed-by-the-chinese-government-and-the-chinese-communist-party-to-the-economic-and-national-security-of-the-united-states.

WWF. 2015. Coal Finance: Will the OECD Lag Behind Emerging Countries because of Japan?: World Wide Fund for Nature.

Yamazaki, Shuji. 2003. 戦後日本の自動車産業政策 *Postwar Japan's Automobile Industry Policy.* Kyoto Hōritsu Bunkasha.

Yang, Zeyi. 2023. "How Did China Come to Dominate the World of Electric Cars?" *MIT Technology Review.* February 21, 2023.

Yasuda, Tetsuji. 2021. Development of Advanced Semiconductor Manufacturing Technology at AIST. Tokyo: AIST.

Zenglein, Max J., and Anna Holzmann. 2019. Evolving Made in China 2025: China's Industrial Policy in the Quest for Global Tech Leadership. Berlin: Mercator Institute for China Studies, MERICS Papers on China No. 8.

Cambridge Elements ☰

Politics and Society in East Asia

Erin Aeran Chung
Johns Hopkins University

Erin Aeran Chung is the Charles D. Miller Professor of East Asian Politics in the Department of Political Science at the Johns Hopkins University. She specializes in East Asian political economy, migration and citizenship, and comparative racial politics. She is the author of *Immigration and Citizenship in Japan* (Cambridge, 2010, 2014; Japanese translation, Akashi Shoten, 2012) and *Immigrant Incorporation in East Asian Democracies* (Cambridge, 2020). Her research has been supported by grants from the Academy of Korean Studies, the Japan Foundation, the Japan Foundation Center for Global Partnership, the Social Science Research Council, and the American Council of Learned Societies.

Mary Alice Haddad
Wesleyan University

Mary Alice Haddad is the John E. Andrus Professor of Government, East Asian Studies, and Environmental Studies at Wesleyan University. Her research focuses on democracy, civil society, and environmental politics in East Asia as well as city diplomacy around the globe. A Fulbright and Harvard Academy scholar, Haddad is author of *Effective Advocacy: Lessons from East Asia's Environmentalists* (MIT, 2021), *Building Democracy in Japan* (Cambridge, 2012), and *Politics and Volunteering in Japan* (Cambridge, 2007), and co-editor of *Greening East Asia* (University of Washington, 2021), and *NIMBY is Beautiful* (Berghahn Books, 2015). She has published in journals such as *Comparative Political Studies, Democratization, Journal of Asian Studies*, and *Nonprofit and Voluntary Sector Quarterly*, with writing for the public appearing in the *Asahi Shimbun*, the *Hartford Courant*, and the *South China Morning Post*.

Benjamin L. Read
University of California, Santa Cruz

Benjamin L. Read is a professor of Politics at the University of California, Santa Cruz. His research has focused on local politics in China and Taiwan, and he also writes about issues and techniques in comparison and field research. He is author of *Roots of the State: Neighborhood Organization and Social Networks in Beijing and Taipei* (Stanford, 2012), coauthor of *Field Research in Political Science: Practices and Principles* (Cambridge, 2015), and co-editor of *Local Organizations and Urban Governance in East and Southeast Asia: Straddling State and Society* (Routledge, 2009). His work has appeared in journals such as *Comparative Political Studies, Comparative Politics, the Journal of Conflict Resolution, the China Journal, the China Quarterly*, and *the Washington Quarterly*, as well as several edited books.

About the Series

The Cambridge Elements series on Politics and Society in East Asia offers original, multidisciplinary contributions on enduring and emerging issues in the dynamic region of East Asia by leading scholars in the field. Suitable for general readers and specialists alike, these short, peer-reviewed volumes examine common challenges and patterns within the region while identifying key differences between countries. The series consists of two types of contributions: 1) authoritative field surveys of established concepts and themes that offer roadmaps for further research; and 2) new research on emerging issues that challenge conventional understandings of East Asian politics and society. Whether focusing on an individual country or spanning the region, the contributions in this series connect regional trends with points of theoretical debate in the social sciences and will stimulate productive interchanges among students, researchers, and practitioners alike.

Cambridge Elements ≡

Politics and Society in East Asia

Elements in the Series

The Digital Transformation and Japan's Political Economy
Ulrike Schaede and Kay Shimizu

Japan as a Global Military Power: New Capabilities, Alliance Integration, Bilateralism-Plus
Christopher W. Hughes

State and Social Protests in China
Yongshun Cai and Chih-Jou Jay Chen

The State and Capitalism in China
Margaret M. Pearson, Meg Rithmire and Kellee Tsai

Political Selection in China: Rethinking Foundations and Findings
Melanie Manion

Environmental Politics in East Asia
Mary Alice Haddad

Politics of the North Korean Diaspora
Sheena Chestnut Greitens

The Adaptability of the Chinese Communist Party
Martin K. Dimitrov

The Welfare State in East Asia
Joseph Wong

Refugee Policies in East Asia
Petrice R. Flowers

Authoritarian Survival and Leadership Succession in North Korea and Beyond
Edward Goldring and Peter Ward

Japan's New Industrial Policy
Gregory W. Noble

A full series listing is available at: www.cambridge.org/EPEA

Printed in the United States
by Baker & Taylor Publisher Services